Rays of Victory Series

My Rays of Victory Bible Study Diary

"There are three things that will endure — faith, hope and love — and the greatest of these is love." (1 Corinthians 13:13)

This Book Belongs to:

_____

(Your Beautiful Name)

God's glory "...covered the heavens, and the earth was full of His praise. His brightness was like the light; He had rays flashing from His hand, and there His power was hidden."
— Habakkuk 3:4

Allow God's glorious rays to shine in and through You!

"There are three things that will endure — faith, hope and love — and the greatest of these is love." (1 Corinthians 13:13)

"I believe the Bible is the best gift God has ever given to men. All the good from the Savior of the world is communicated to us through this book."

President Abraham Lincoln

"There are three things that will endure — faith, hope and love — and the greatest of these is love." (1 Corinthians 13:13)

My Rays of Victory

Bible Study

Diary

"There are three things that will endure — faith, hope and love — and the greatest of these is love." (1 Corinthians 13:13)

We are in His Image

Regardless of race, ethnicity or nationality we are all created in the Image of God.

"So God created human beings in his image. In the image of God he created them. He created them male and female."

— Genesis 1:27 (NCV)

"There are three things that will endure — faith, hope and love — and the greatest of these is love." (1 Corinthians 13:13)

"Those who deny freedom to others deserve it not for themselves; and, under a just God, cannot long retain it."
— **President Abraham Lincoln**

"As I have said, the first thing is to be honest with yourself. You can never have an impact on society if you have not changed yourself... Great peacemakers are all people of integrity, of honesty, but humility."
— **President Nelson Mandela**

"Believe in justice and freedom for all and work actively for it."
— **Jacyee Aniagolu-Johnson**

"There are three things that will endure — faith, hope and love — and the greatest of these is love." (1 Corinthians 13:13)

Copyright Permission

"*My Rays of Victory Bible Study Diary*" Copyright 2002-2013, Jacinta Aniagolu (Jacyee Aniagolu-Johnson). A Marble Tower Publishing "*Rays of Victory Bible Study Diary*" book publication. Publishing rights owned by Marble Tower Publishing, LLC. Unauthorized duplication is prohibited by law and the eighth commandment.

No part of this book may be reproduced, stored in a retrieval system, or transmitted by any means, electronic, mechanical, photocopying, recording, or otherwise, without written permission from the author.

Churches and other non-commercial interests such as non-profit organizations may quote text from this Diary book without written permission of Marble Tower Publishing, provided that the text does not exceed 500 words of the entire book and the text is not material quoted from another publisher or author. When quoting text from this book please include the following credit line: "From *My Rays of Victory Bible Study Diary* by Jacyee Aniagolu-Johnson, published by Marble Tower Publishing, LLC. Used by permission.

First Paperback Edition
ISBN: 978-0-9789669-4-2 / 0-9789669-4-5 (pbk.)

Printed in the United States of America
Marble Tower Publishing, LLC.

"There are three things that will endure — faith, hope and love — and the greatest of these is love." (1 Corinthians 13:13)

Edited by Uché Aniagolu (Ebony Woodhouse Productions, LLC)

Cover design by Marble Tower Publishing, LLC
Cover Image Source: Online Microsoft Clip Art Gallery (Open Source)

First Paperback Edition
ISBN 978-0-9789669-4-2 / 0-9789669-4-5 (pbk.)

Printed in the United States of America by Marble Tower Publishing, LLC (www.marbletowerpublishing.com)

Our motto: Empowering minds to create wealth and creating wealth to do God's work.

"*My Rays of Victory Bible Study Diary*" Published by Marble Tower Publishing, LLC. All rights reserved.

Scripture quotation is taken from:

The HOLY BIBLE, KING JAMES VERSION, Cambridge, 1769. (Public Domain).

The Holy Bible, New Century Version® (NCV) Copyright © 2005 by Thomas Nelson, Inc.

New International Reader's Version (NIRV) Copyright © 1996, 1998 by International Bible Society

New King James Version (NKJV) Copyright © 1982 by Thomas Nelson, Inc.

New International Version (NIV) Copyright © 1973, 1978, 1984, 2010 by International Bible Society

---

"There are three things that will endure — faith, hope and love — and the greatest of these is love." (1 Corinthians 13:13)

Please send Correspondence to:

Marble Tower Publishing, LLC
P.O. Box 1654
Laurel, Maryland 20725, USA.

You may also contact us via our websites:
www.marbletowerpublishing.com
www.ravbookseries.com

"There are three things that will endure — faith, hope and love — and the greatest of these is love." (1 Corinthians 13:13)

Dedication

My Rays of Victory Bible Study Diary

This book is dedicated to God Almighty who is our Heavenly Father, His Holy Spirit, and His only Son, our Lord and Savior Jesus Christ, Who died for all of us so that we may have eternal salvation (John 3:16); and to you the owner of this book.

"There are three things that will endure — faith, hope and love — and the greatest of these is love." (1 Corinthians 13:13)

You, Me and Us!

Our Individual and Collective Power to Effect Positive Change

"We (Black, White, Hispanic and Latino, Asian, Mixed Race, and every race of human beings) are all created in the perfect Image of God (Genesis 1:26-27). Individually and collectively, without division or hostility, we have the power of God in us to effect change and the change we seek daily in our world must start with us reflecting that change in our individual lives; then in our families and communities; and in our states and countries; and that change will spread like wildfire to touch every part of the world."

Jacyee Aniagolu-Johnson

"There are three things that will endure — faith, hope and love — and the greatest of these is love." (1 Corinthians 13:13)

Acknowledgements

My utmost gratitude goes to our Heavenly Father, Triune God Almighty who has the power to save all, regardless of race, ethnicity or nationality—for His glorious rays of victory over racism. I love you awesome Father with all my spirit, soul and body.

To my dear dad, Justice Anthony Aniagolu and my mom Lady Maria Aniagolu whom I love dearly for being wonderful parents and for all that they have done for me and my siblings.

For honoring God's love for me and my love for Him, my love and warm gratitude goes to my husband, Lamonte Johnson. I love you very much.

My special gratitude also goes to my sister, Maryanne, a lovely woman of God—thank you for continuing to help me to better understand how to hear the true voice of God and how to spend endless quality time in God's Holy Presence through prayer, thanksgiving and worship. I love you very much.

"There are three things that will endure — faith, hope and love — and the greatest of these is love." (1 Corinthians 13:13)

To my sister Uché, I thank God for the sweet fragrance of Christ in you. You are an embodiment of servanthood and selfless sacrificial giving, and it is the greatness of God in you through Jesus Christ that empowers you to humble yourself to serve others. I have no doubt that God will magnify His glory in your life through Jesus Christ. I love you very much.

To my sister Chi-Chi who's giving spirit surpasses anyone that I know. May Luke 6:38 remain like a wellspring within you and may God continue to bless you and enrich your life beyond your wildest imagination through Jesus Christ! I love you very much.

To my brother Kizito whose deep and genuine love for God helps me to stay focused on Matthew 6:33; may the power of God's Holy Word continue to promote you from faith to faith and from glory to glory, in the awesome Name of our Lord and Savior Jesus Christ. I love you very much.

To the rest of my family, Tony, Emeka, Chuka, Lolly and Nwachu, I remain forever grateful to God for your lives, individual families and accomplishments. It is my prayer that John 3:16 will be and remain alive in your hearts. I love you very much.

"There are three things that will endure — faith, hope and love — and the greatest of these is love." (1 Corinthians 13:13)

Finally, to my friends and prayer partners, and the Body of Jesus Christ as a whole (all believers in Him and all of God's true priests and ministers around the world), regardless of denomination, may God's favor and blessings always overflow in your lives as you continue to spread the good news of the Gospel of our Lord and Savior, Jesus Christ, and further His powerful ministry, firmly rooted in true and pure Love, which is God the Father Himself.

"There are three things that will endure — faith, hope and love — and the greatest of these is love." (1 Corinthians 13:13)

Prayer of Salvation

On this day, _____, I, _____ confess with my mouth that the Lord Jesus Christ is my personal Lord and Savior; I believe He shed His Blood for me on the Cross of Calvary and that God raised Him from the dead for my eternal salvation. I repent of my sins and ask God for forgiveness through the mighty Blood of Jesus Christ.

On this day, _____ by my faith, I, _____ believe that I am now saved by the precious Blood of Jesus Christ. I believe in the Triune God: God the Father, God the Son, Jesus Christ, and God the Holy Spirit. I believe that in the Name of our Lord and Savior Jesus Christ and through the anointing by God's Holy Spirit, I will receive the baptism of God's Holy Spirit that will release from my heart the flowing rivers of living water, in Jesus' Name, Amen.

Thank you Father, Lord God, for on this day, _____, in the Name of Jesus Christ, I, _____ am Born Again!

"There are three things that will endure — faith, hope and love — and the greatest of these is love." (1 Corinthians 13:13)

Scripture Meditation:

"For God so loved the world that He gave His only begotten Son, that whoever believes in Him should not perish but have everlasting life."
— John 3:16

"But what does it say? 'The word is near you, in your mouth and in your heart' (that is, the word of faith which we preach): that if you confess with your mouth the Lord Jesus and believe in your heart that God has raised Him from the dead, you will be saved. For with the heart one believes unto righteousness, and with the mouth confession is made unto salvation."
— Romans 10:8-9

"He who believes in Me, as the Scripture has said, out of his heart will flow rivers of living water."
— John 7:38

"That which is born of the flesh is flesh, and that which is born of the Spirit is spirit. Do not marvel that I said to you, 'You must be born-again.'"
— John 3:6-7

"There are three things that will endure — faith, hope and love — and the greatest of these is love." (1 Corinthians 13:13)

Prayer after Profession of Salvation

Dear Glorious Heavenly Father, thank You that I am born again by the precious Blood of Jesus Christ. I accept my renewed spirit in Him.

Dear gracious Father, I thank You for making me aware that I have spiritual and mental shackles from my experiences with racism. Thank You for revealing to me all areas where I am shackled. Thank You for giving me total release and freedom from the intrigues of the foul spirit of racism. I reject the evil tradition of racism and all that it stands for. I forgive anyone who has hurt or offended me in any manner, including my racist offenders.

Dear precious Father, I believe that You have answered my prayers in the precious Name of Jesus Christ. In the Name of Jesus Christ and by Your enabling grace, Lord God, I know that I can and that I have gained victory over any form of racial oppression and injustice.

Thank You, awesome Father, for Your marvelous rays of victory over racism on my behalf, and for Your limitless and boundless power within me through Jesus Christ, Amen.

"There are three things that will endure — faith, hope and love — and the greatest of these is love." (1 Corinthians 13:13)

Scripture Meditation:

"And whatever you ask in My name, I will do, that the Father may be glorified in the Son. If you ask anything in My name, I will do it." – John 14:13-14

"Pray without ceasing; in everything give thanks; for this is the will of God in Jesus Christ for you." – 1 Thessalonians 5:17-18

"And whenever you stand praying, if you have anything against anyone, forgive him that your Father in heaven may also forgive you your trespasses." – Mark 11:25

"Until now you have asked nothing in My name. Ask and you will receive, that your joy may be full." – John 16:24

"Don't copy the behavior and customs of this world, but let God transform you into a new person by changing the way you think. Then you will learn to know God's will for you, which is good and pleasing and perfect." – Romans 12:2

"There are three things that will endure — faith, hope and love — and the greatest of these is love." (1 Corinthians 13:13)

Partnership Prayer

I commit to spending quality time in prayer, worship and thanksgiving, and meditating on God's Holy Word, to receive His powerful and winning strategies for my daily victory over racism. This I shall do only by the grace of God, in the Name of our Lord and Savior Jesus Christ and through daily guidance by the Holy Spirit. I stand in agreement with my prayer partner(s) _____ believing that through the redeeming precious Blood of Jesus Christ, God has taken away the burden of racism, its reproach and yoke of destruction from all areas of my life. I stand in agreement with my prayer partner(s) _____ believing that the precious Blood of Jesus Christ has permanently destroyed and removed the power of the burden of the foul spirit of racism in my life, in Jesus' Name, Amen.

_____

Your Name

_____

Prayer Partner's Name

"There are three things that will endure — faith, hope and love — and the greatest of these is love." (1 Corinthians 13:13)

Jacyee Aniagolu Johnson

Dr. Jacyee Aniagolu-Johnson

(Author remains in agreement with you)

"Again I say to you that if two of you agree on earth concerning anything that they ask, it will be done for them by My Father in heaven."
– Matthew 18:19

"It shall come to pass in that day that his burden will be taken away from your shoulder, and his yoke from your neck, and the yoke will be destroyed because of the anointing oil."
– Isaiah 10:27

"There are three things that will endure — faith, hope and love — and the greatest of these is love." (1 Corinthians 13:13)

Contents

Dedication 10

You, Me and Us! 11

Acknowledgements 12

Prayer of Salvation 15

Prayer after Profession of Salvation 17

Partnership Prayer 19

Hebrew Names of God and their Meanings 23

Who God is – The "I AM's" of God 24

Daily Living Bible Meditation Verses 25

Dealing with Racism? 33

"There are three things that will endure — faith, hope and love — and the greatest of these is love." (1 Corinthians 13:13)

Personal Diary Entry Notes *35*

Personal Inspiration Entry Notes *72*

Personal Revelation Entry Notes *93*

Bible Reading Schedule *124*

Bible Study Entry Notes *128*

General Notes *147*

Power Thoughts Against Racism *177*

Personal Journey Entry Notes *206*

Personal Journey Entry Notes *207*

Nailing Racism to the Cross *222*

"There are three things that will endure — faith, hope and love — and the greatest of these is love." (1 Corinthians 13:13)

Hebrew Names of God and their Meanings

[Reference: "Names of God" by Lambert Dolphin (www.ldolphin.org) Used with Permission.]

Adonai-Jehovah -- The Lord our Sovereign

El-Elyon -- The Lord Most High

El-Olam -- The Everlasting God

El-Shaddai -- The God Who is Sufficient…

Jehovah-Elohim -- The Eternal Creator

Jehovah-Jireh -- The Lord our Provider

Jehovah-Nissi -- The Lord our Banner

Jehovah-Ropheka -- The Lord our Healer

Jehovah-Shalom -- The Lord our Peace

Jehovah-Tsidkenu -- The Lord our Righteousness

Jehovah-Mekaddishkem -- The Lord our Sanctifier

Jehovah-Sabaoth -- The Lord of Hosts

Jehovah-Shammah -- The Lord is Present

Jehovah-Rohi -- The Lord our Shepherd

Jehovah-Hoseenu -- The Lord our Maker

Jehovah-Eloheenu -- The Lord our God

(There are many more names of God…visit www.ldolphin.org)

"There are three things that will endure — faith, hope and love — and the greatest of these is love." (1 Corinthians 13:13)

Who God is – The "I AM's" of God

(Compiled by: www.characterbuildingforfamilies.com
based on the King James Bible Version)

I AM

I AM THAT I AM

I AM a Father to Israel

I AM a Great King

I AM Alive Forevermore

I AM Alpha and Omega

I AM for you

I AM from Above

I AM God

I AM God Almighty

I AM Gracious

I AM He that comforts you

(And many more Names...For a comprehensive list of "I AM" Names of God, visit www.characterbuildingforfamilies.com, copyright owner of the booklet "Names of God" which contains 600 Names of God and "I AM" Names.)

"There are three things that will endure — faith, hope and love — and the greatest of these is love." (1 Corinthians 13:13)

Daily Living Bible Meditation Verses

Doubting God?	Seeking God's Will or Direction?	Holding onto God?
Isaiah 26:3, 12	John 14:16-17	Psalms 3:26
Isaiah 55:10-11	John 16:13	Psalms 18:30
Isaiah 59:1	Isaiah 58:11	Psalms 34:19
Psalms 18:30	Proverbs 3:5-6	Psalms 46
Psalms 27	Psalms 31:3	Psalms 91
Psalms 91:14-15	Proverbs 16:3	Psalms 138:8
2 Peter 3:9	Psalms 48:14	Isaiah 55:8-9
Isaiah 46: 10b, 11b	Psalms 37:23	Hebrews 10:23
Romans 4:20-21	Isaiah 30:21	Romans 8:28
1 Thessalonians 5:24	Isaiah 48:17	Isaiah 41:10
Luke 12:29-31	Proverbs 6:22-23	Psalms 55:22
Mark 11:22-24	Psalms 27:1-3	1 Corinthians 10:13
Psalms 23	Psalms 40:2-3	Romans 8:31, 35-37
Psalms 119:105	Psalms 32:8	Jeremiah 32:40-41, 33:3
James 1:5	Psalms 119:105	Hebrews 10:35-37
Hebrew 6:10	Jeremiah 6:16	Joshua 1:9
Jeremiah 29:11	Jeremiah 33:3	
Hebrews 11:6	Psalms 32:8	
2 Corinthians 5:17	Isaiah 30:20-21	
	James 1:5	
Dealing with Trials?	**Facing Financial Problems?**	**Feeling Discouraged?**
Psalms 69:14-18	Deuteronomy 8:18,	Psalms 27:1-3
Job 13: 15-16	Deuteronomy 28:1-15	Psalms 40:2-3
Isaiah 43:2-3		Psalms 138:7
James 1:12		Isaiah 51:11

"There are three things that will endure — faith, hope and love — and the greatest of these is love." (1 Corinthians 13:13)

Psalms 18:28-30, 32 Psalms 34:17-19 Psalms 40:2-3 Job 23:10-11 1 Peter 4:12-13, 16 Isaiah 26:3-4 Proverbs 3:5-6 Psalms 27:1-3	Psalms 37:3-4 Psalms 40:2-3 Luke 12:22-24 Hebrews 13:6 1 Timothy 6:17-19 Philippians 4:11-13, 19 Proverbs 3:5-6	1 Peter 1:6-9 John 14:1 Philippians 4:6-8 Joshua 1:9 Isaiah 26:3-4, 51:11 Isaiah 40:1-2 Isaiah 61
Need to Forgive or be Forgiven?	**Dealing with Anger?**	**Are you Afraid?**
Matthew 5:10-12 Hebrews 10:30 Isaiah 43:18-19 Philippians 3:13-14 Colossians 1:13-14 Colossians 3:13-14 Matthew 6:14-15 Matthew 18: 21-22 Luke 17:3-4 Mark 11:25 Matthew 5:44-45 1 John 1:8-10 Acts 3:19 1 John 1:9 Isaiah 43:25-26 Acts 3:19 Isaiah 1:18 Ephesians 1:7 Hebrews 10:17 Daniel 9:9 Micah 7:18-19 Psalms 86:15	Psalms 37:8 Psalms 145:8 Ecclesiastes 7:8-9 Romans 12:19 Proverbs 16:32 Proverbs 14:17, 29 Proverbs 19:11 Proverbs 25: 21-22 Matthew 5:22, 6:14 Proverbs 12:16 Proverbs 14:17,15:1,18 Ephesians 4:26, 29-32 James 1:19-20 James 4:7 Colossians 3:8 1 Thessalonians 5:8 Nehemiah 9:17 Proverbs 29:11	Psalms 23:1-6 Psalms 27:1-5 Psalms 31:24 Psalms 35:1-28 Psalms 37:1-40 Psalms 56:11 Psalms 91:1-7, 10-11 Exodus 14:13 Isaiah 54:14-15 1 John 4:18 Proverbs 3:25-26 Romans 8:15 2 Timothy 1:7 Joshua 1:7-9 Isaiah 41:10 Isaiah 43:1-3, 5, 7 Isaiah 51:7-8 1 John 4:18 Hebrews 13:6 Jeremiah 1:19 2 Chronicles 20:17

"There are three things that will endure — faith, hope and love — and the greatest of these is love." (1 Corinthians 13:13)

Needing Courage?	Needing Patience?	Needing Confidence?
Psalms 31:24	Isaiah 26:3, 12	Hebrews 11:6
Philippians 4:13	Isaiah 55:11	Hebrews 10-35-36
Psalms 118:17	Isaiah 40:31	Philippians 1:6
Deuteronomy 33:27	Galatians 5:22, 6:9	Philippians 4:13
Isaiah 41:10	Colossians 3:12-13	Habakkuk 3:19
Romans 8:25	James 1:3-4, 19-20	1 John 5:14-15
Romans 8:38-39	James 5:7-8	Isaiah 43:2
1 Peter 4:12-13	Hebrews 6:12	Zechariah 4:6
Psalms 27:14	Lamentations 3:26	Proverbs 3:5-6
Hebrews 13:6	Romans 8:24-25	Proverbs 3:26
1 John 3:21	Romans 15:4-5	2 Corinthians 7:16
Joshua 1:7-9	Psalms 37:7-9	Ephesians 3:12
Psalms 31:24	Psalms 40:1	I John 5:14
Psalms 37:3	Ephesians 4:1-2	John 14:12
Psalms 56:3-4	Romans 5:3, 15:5	Isaiah 26:1-4
Proverbs 3:5-6	Romans 12:12	Romans 8:37
Psalms 91:1-3	Romans 15:4-5	Psalms 23:1-6
Psalms 23:1-6	Psalms 27:13-14	Psalms 91:1-7
Psalms 27:1-5	Psalms 37:7-9	Psalms 37:1-40
Jeremiah 1:19	Psalms 91:1-7	
	Psalms 116:1-9	
Waiting on God?	**Building your Faith?**	**What about Love?**
Psalms 145-15-16	Hebrews 11:1	John 3:16
Psalms 130:5	1 John 5:4	Romans 8:38-39
Hebrews 10:23	James 5:14-15	Romans 5:8
Habakkuk 2:3	Matthew 9:28-29	Jeremiah 31:3
Isaiah 40:29, 31	Matthew 9:20-22	John 14:21
Psalms 62:5	Romans 10:17	John 16:27
Psalms 33:20	1 Peter 1:7-9	1 Corinthians 13:1-8, 13
Hebrews 3:14	Mark 9:23	
Psalms 27:14	Hebrews 11:6	John 15:9-10

"There are three things that will endure — faith, hope and love — and the greatest of these is love." (1 Corinthians 13:13)

Isaiah 43:1 2 Kings 6:16 Isaiah 40:29-31	Mark 11:22-24 Hebrews 13:8	1 John 4:10-12 1 John 4:7-8 Romans 13:8
In Need of Peace?	**Feeling Alone?**	**Grieving?**
Philippians 4:6-7 2 Corinthians 13:11 Romans 14:17-19 Romans 5:1 Romans 8:6 Romans 15:13 Isaiah 26:3-4, 12 Isaiah 55:12 Isaiah 57:2 John 14:27 John 16:33 John 20:19 Proverbs 16:7 Ephesians 6:23 2 Thessalonians 3:16 Isaiah 57:18-19 Isaiah 61:1-3 Psalms 1:1-6 Psalms 3:1-8 Psalms 4:1,8 Psalms 23 Psalms 27 Psalms 29:11 Psalms 37:11,37 Psalms 91 Psalms 119:165 Colossians 3:15 Matthew 5:9 Matthew 11:28-30	Deuteronomy 31:6-8 Psalms 23 Psalms 27 Psalms 91 Psalms 43:5 Isaiah 49: 15-16 Isaiah 41:17 Psalms 91:14-15; 94:14 Psalms 37:25 1 Peter 5:7 2 Corinthians 4:9 Deuteronomy 4:31 Matthew 28:20 Psalms 9:10; 27:10 Hebrews 13:5 1 Samuel 12:22 Matthew 28:20 1 Samuel 12:22 John 14: 1, 18 Deuteronomy 33:27 Deuteronomy 4:31 Isaiah 61:1-3 Isaiah 57:18-19 Joshua 1:7-9 Hebrews 6:15, 19 Psalms 103:10-12	1 Thessalonians 4:13-14 Isaiah 49:13b Isaiah 57:18-19 Isaiah 61:1-3 Matthew 5:4 2 Corinthians 1:3-4 Psalms 23 Psalms 91 Psalms 119:50 1 Corinthians 15:55-57 Psalms 23:4 Deuteronomy 4:31 Revelation 21:4 1 Peter 5:7 Isaiah 14:3-6 Isaiah 41:10 Psalms 119:165 Psalms 31:3,9 Psalms 34:18 Psalms 71:21 Proverbs 3:5 Isaiah 51:11 Psalms 71:20 John 11:40 1 Peter 1:6-9

"There are three things that will endure — faith, hope and love — and the greatest of these is love." (1 Corinthians 13:13)

Problems in your Marriage?	Feeling Dissatisfied with Life?	Feeling Condemned?
Proverbs 3:5-6　　　　　　　Proverbs 10:12　　　　　　　Psalms 101:2　　　　　　　　1 Peter 3:8-11　　　　　　　Romans 13:10　　　　　　　 1 Peter 3:1-7　　　　　　　　Joshua 24:15　　　　　　　　Genesis 2:18　　　　　　　　Genesis 2:24　　　　　　　　Ephesians 4:31-32　　　　　Ephesians 4:26　　　　　　　Ephesians 6:10-18　　　　　Matthew 19:5-6　　　　　　Matthew 19:26　　　　　　　1 Peter 1:6-9　　　　　　　　Matthew 11:28-30	Psalms 40:1-17　　　　　　Psalms 103:2-5　　　　　　 2 Corinthians 9:8　　　　　Isaiah 55:1　　　　　　　　 Psalms 107:9　　　　　　　 Psalms 37:3　　　　　　　　Matthew 5:6　　　　　　　　Psalms 63:1-5　　　　　　　Philippians 4:12-13　　　　Proverbs 12:14　　　　　　 Isaiah 44:3　　　　　　　　 Psalms 34:10　　　　　　　 1 Peter 1:6-9　　　　　　　 Matthew 11:28-30　　　　 Psalms 42:1-11	Hebrews 10:22　　　　　　Psalms 32:1　　　　　　　　1 John 1:9　　　　　　　　Psalms 32:5　　　　　　　　Isaiah 55:7; 43:25　　　　Hebrews 8:12　　　　　　　John 5:24　　　　　　　　　John 3:17-18　　　　　　　2 Corinthians 5:17　　　　Psalms 103:10-12　　　　　Romans 8:1　　　　　　　　Romans 8:35-39　　　　　 Psalms 23:1-6　　　　　　　Psalms 18:1-50　　　　　　Psalms 40:1-17　　　　　　Psalms 44:1-26
Your Total Allegiance to God?	**Your Obedience to God?**	**The Power of God's Grace?**
Psalms 100:2　　　　　　　Joshua, 22:5; 24:15　　　　Exodus 23:25-26　　　　　 Romans 12:10-13　　　　　Deuteronomy 10:12, 13:4　　　　　　　　　　　Deuteronomy 13:4　　　　 Romans 12:1-2　　　　　　Matthew 4:10　　　　　　　Matthew 6:24　　　　　　　Luke 10:27	Deuteronomy 5:1, 32-33　　　　　　　　　　　Psalms 143:10　　　　　　 1 Kings 3:14　　　　　　　 Acts 5:29　　　　　　　　　1 John 2:3-6　　　　　　　 Jeremiah 7:23　　　　　　　Isaiah 1:19　　　　　　　　 Isaiah 48:18　　　　　　　 John 14:15, 21　　　　　　1 Samuel 15:22	Hebrews 4:16　　　　　　　Ephesians 1:6　　　　　　　2 Corinthians 4:15　　　　Proverbs 8:35; 14:9　　　　Proverbs 10:6, 22, 24　　　　　　　　　　 Psalms 30:7; 5:12　　　　　Psalms 84:11　　　　　　　 Job 10:12

"There are three things that will endure — faith, hope and love — and the greatest of these is love." (1 Corinthians 13:13)

Matthew 22:37 Psalms 27 Psalms 91 Psalms 147:11 2 Corinthians 2:16-17 Revelation 1:3	Deuteronomy 11:26-28 Romans 2:13 2 Corinthians 10:5 John 14:23 2 Corinthians 2:16-17	Exodus 33:17 Ephesians 2:6-10 Isaiah 60:10 Titus 2:11-15 2 Corinthians 12:8-9 Romans 3:20-24
Received God's Holy Spirit?	**The Power of God's Holy Spirit?**	**Knowing the Power of God's Holy Word?**
Matthew 28:19 John 20:22 Acts 1:4,5,8 Acts 2:38 John 14:16-17, 26 Joel 2:28 Matthew 3:11 Acts 2:4 John 16: 7,13 Luke 11:13 Luke 12:12 John 7:38,39 Romans 5,5 1 Corinthians 6:19 Luke 11:9-13 Acts 7:55 Acts 9:17 Acts 19:6 Acts 10:45 John 7:38-39 Romans 5:5 John 7:38-39 Hebrews 12:25	Luke 11:13 Luke 12:12 Luke 24:49 Jude 20, 21 2 Peter 1:20-21 Isaiah 59:19 Luke 12:12 Matthew 10:20 Galatians 5:22-25 2 Corinthians 3:6, 17-18 Hebrews 12:25 Acts 1:4-8 Acts 2:4 Acts 2:33 Acts 2:38 Acts 7:55 Acts 10:38 Acts 10:44-46 John 16:7-14 John 14:16-18,22-26 Romans 15:19	Mark 12:24 John 1:1 John 8:31-32 John 14:9-11 1 Peter 1:23-25 Matthew 4:4 Isaiah 40:8 John 6:63, 15:3 Psalms 33:6 Psalms 119:89-90 Hebrews 4:12-13 1 Peter 2:2-3 Psalms 119: 11,16 John 15:26 Acts 13:52 Acts 15:8 Deuteronomy 28:1-14 Ephesians 6:17,19 James 1:18 Revelation 22:6,18-20

"There are three things that will endure — faith, hope and love — and the greatest of these is love." (1 Corinthians 13:13)

Focusing on Spiritual Things?	Overcoming Worldliness?	Struggling with Pride?
Acts 4:13	Luke 21:34	Proverbs 15:33; 16:18-20
Acts 19:1-6	1 John 2:15-17	Proverbs 28:25-26
Romans 5:5	Joshua 24:14	Matthew 11:29-30
Romans 8:2-11	Romans 12:2	Jeremiah 13:15-17
Romans 15:13	Romans 13:11-14	2 Corinthians 4:7
Colossians 2:8	2 Peter 1:4	1 Peter 5:5-6
Galatians 2:20	Luke 9:23-25	Matthew 20:26-27
1 Corinthians 2:13-14	Matthew 6:24	James 4:6-7, 10
2 Corinthians 4:16	Romans 12:2	Matthew 18:2-4
1 Peter 1:13-15	2 Peter 2:9	1 John 2:16
Romans 12:1-2	Titus 2:11-15	
Deuteronomy 8:3	Matthew 4:4	
Galatians 5:13-21	Deuteronomy 8:3	
Matthew 6:19-20	Deuteronomy 8:18	
	Hebrews 13:5	

Handling Stress?	Overcoming Despair?	Trying to Maintain Hope?
Psalms 56:3-4	Galatians 6:9	Matthew 6:34
Mark 4:38-40	Hebrews 6:15, 19	1 Thessalonians 5:8-9
John 14:27	Hebrews 13:5-6	Lamentations 3:21-24
Psalms 46:1-3	Psalms 103:10-12	Psalms 27:14
1 Peter 5:7-10	Philippians 4:8	Psalms 42:5
Psalms 23:2-4	Romans 8:28	Psalms 119:14
Psalms 91:3-7	2 Corinthians 4:8-9	Psalms 33:18-22
Ephesians 4:26-17	2 Corinthians 4:16-18	Hebrews 13:5-6
Isaiah 41:10	Matthew 11:28	Romans 15:13
Philippians 4:6-8	Psalms 30:5, 8-12	Psalms 55:22
Matthew 11:28	Psalms 23, 91	Psalms 62:5-7
Psalms 18	Psalms 27	Isaiah 40:31
Psalms 35	Psalms 43:5	Psalms 147:11
Psalms 37	Isaiah 61:1-3	Psalms 42
Psalms 42		

"There are three things that will endure — faith, hope and love — and the greatest of these is love." (1 Corinthians 13:13)

Psalms 144 Psalms 147:11	Isaiah 57:18-19 Joshua 1:7-9	Psalms 43 Micah 7:7
Facing Serious Illness?	**Handling Suffering?**	**Entering God's Rest?**
Psalms 23:4 Psalms 48:14 Psalms 49:15 Psalms 91 2 Corinthians 5:1 Psalms 118:17-18 John 11:3-4 John 11:40 2 Corinthians 4:16-18 1 Peter 2:24 Jeremiah 17:14 James 5:14-15 Isaiah 26:3-4 Jeremiah 30:17 Isaiah 53:5 Isaiah 61:1-3	Romans 8:17-18 Hebrews 2:9-10 1 Peter 2:20-21 James 1:12 Hebrews 12:6-8, 11-13 2 Timothy 2-3 1 Peter 4:1-2, 12-17 Philippians 4:19 Proverbs 13:7,11 Hebrews 10:36 Isaiah 61:1-3 Psalms 37:3-4 Matthew 10:38 Psalms 103:1-3 Psalms 30:5	Proverbs 29:35 1 Corinthians 14:33 2 Corinthians 1:9-10 Romans 8:28 Romans 5:1-2 Exodus 33:14 Hebrews 4:9, 11,14 Psalms 37:5-7 Jeremiah 17:7-8 1 Peter 5:7 Psalms 46:2 Matthew 11:28 Isaiah 26:3 Isaiah 61:10

"There are three things that will endure — faith, hope and love — and the greatest of these is love." (1 Corinthians 13:13)

Dealing with Racism?

Exodus 3:7-21

Exodus 14:13-14

Isaiah 54:13-15

Psalms 23, 27, 35, 37, 59, 91

Jeremiah 51:20

Acts 7:30-38

2 Corinthians 4:1-18

Ephesians 6:10-18

1 Peter 3:8-16

"There are three things that will endure — faith, hope and love — and the greatest of these is love." (1 Corinthians 13:13)

Bible Inspirational Quotes

"Remember that I commanded you to be strong and brave. Don't be afraid, because the LORD your God will be with you everywhere you go."

Joshua 1:9 (NCV)

"Be on your guard; stand firm in the faith; be men of courage; be strong."

1 Corinthians 16:13 (NIV)

"But even if you should suffer for what is right, you are blessed. "Do not fear their threats; do not be frightened."

1 Peter 3:14 (NIV)

"So do not fear, for I am with you; do not be dismayed, for I am your God. I will strengthen you and help you; I will uphold you with my righteous right hand."

Isaiah 41:10 (NIV)

"There are three things that will endure — faith, hope and love — and the greatest of these is love." (1 Corinthians 13:13)

Personal Diary Entry Notes

"There are three things that will endure — faith, hope and love — and the greatest of these is love." (1 Corinthians 13:13)

Date:_____

**Title of
Entry:**_____

_____

Love God above all things:

"You shall love the LORD your God with all your heart, with all your soul, and with all your strength." Deuteronomy 6:5 (NKJV) *"Here is what it means to love God. It means that we obey his commands. And his commands are not hard to obey. That's because everyone who is a child of God has won the battle over the world. Our faith has won the battle for us."* 1 John 5:3-4 (NIRV)

_____

Date:_____

Title of
Entry:_____

_____

Receive Jesus Christ; Believe in Him and love Him, for He is the Son of God who died so that you may receive eternal salvation:

"God loved the world so much that he gave his one and only Son. Anyone who believes in him will not die but will have eternal life." John 3:16 (NIRV)

_____

"There are three things that will endure — faith, hope and love — and the greatest of these is love." (1 Corinthians 13:13)

Date:_____

Title of
Entry:_____

_____

Believe in Jesus Christ knowing that the power of God in you through Him has made you a victor (and not a victim):

"Yet in all these things we are more than conquerors through Him who loved us." Romans 8:37 (NKJV)

_____

"There are three things that will endure — faith, hope and love — and the greatest of these is love." (1 Corinthians 13:13)

Date:_____

Title of
Entry:_____

_____

Influence the world around you and be a positive light to those who cross your path, regardless of race, ethnicity or nationality:

"You are the light that gives light to the world. A city that is built on a hill cannot be hidden. And people don't hide a light under a bowl. They put it on a lampstand so the light shines for all the people in the house." Matthew 5:14-15 (NCV)

_____

"There are three things that will endure — faith, hope and love — and the greatest of these is love." (1 Corinthians 13:13)

Date:_____

Title of
Entry:_____

_____

Resist negative change and embrace positive change. Reject the spirit of racism. Receive and support justice and equity for all people, regardless of race or ethnicity:

"Do not be shaped by this world; instead be changed within by a new way of thinking. Then you will be able to decide what God wants for you; you will know what is good and pleasing to him and what is perfect." Romans 12:2 (NCV)

_____

"There are three things that will endure — faith, hope and love — and the greatest of these is love." (1 Corinthians 13:13)

Date:_____

Title of
Entry:_____

_____

Be empowered by God to be a part of change that touches the lives of people in a positive manner. Rosa Parks did it; Reverend (Dr.) Martin Luther King Jr. did it; President Nelson Mandela did it; Blessed Mother Teresa did it, and so can you!

"Do I need to give more examples? I do not have time to tell you about Gideon, Barak, Samson, Jephthah, David, Samuel, and the prophets. Through their faith they defeated kingdoms. They did what was right, received God's promises, and shut the mouths of lions." Hebrews 11:32-33 (NCV)

_____

"There are three things that will endure — faith, hope and love — and the greatest of these is love." (1 Corinthians 13:13)

Date:_____

Title of
Entry:_____

_____

Discard the spirit of selfishness. Be to others what you want others to be to you. Refuse to be an instrument of racism to be used against any individual, ethnic group, race or nationality:

"Do to others as you would have them do to you." Luke 6:31 (NIV) *"The wise people will shine like the brightness of the sky. Those who teach others to live right will shine like stars forever and ever." Daniel 12:3 (NCV)*

_____

"There are three things that will endure — faith, hope and love — and the greatest of these is love." (1 Corinthians 13:13)

Date:_____

Title of
Entry:_____

_____

God is the Chief Executive Officer of your workplace and your life. Let your daily work be pleasing to God who rewards good work:

"Work at everything you do with all your heart. Work as if you were working for the Lord, not for human masters. Work because you know that you will finally receive as a reward what the Lord wants you to have. You are serving the Lord Christ." Colossians 3:23-24 (NIRV)

_____

"There are three things that will endure — faith, hope and love — and the greatest of these is love." (1 Corinthians 13:13)

Date:_____

Title of
Entry:_____

_____

Be a blessing to many; be like a seed that is planted by a stream and which grows into a mighty tree that brings forth its fruit in its season that feeds many; a mustard seed that grows to become a giant tree:

"Another parable He put forth to them, saying: "The kingdom of heaven is like a mustard seed, which a man took and sowed in his field, which indeed is the least of all the seeds; but when it is grown it is greater than the herbs and becomes a tree, so that the birds of the air come and nest in its branches." Matthew 13:32 (NKJV)

_____

"There are three things that will endure — faith, hope and love — and the greatest of these is love." (1 Corinthians 13:13)

Date:_____

Title of Entry:_____

_____

Be grateful and thankful for what you have always. Be grateful and thankful for your ethnicity, race, or nationality; be who God created you to be and says you are in Jesus Christ, and not what someone else calls you or wants you to be:

"Always give thanks to God the Father for everything. Give thanks to him in the name of our Lord Jesus Christ." Ephesians 5:20 (NIRV) *"Yet to all who did receive him, to those who believed in his name, he gave the right to become children of God"* John 1:12 (NIV)

_____

"There are three things that will endure — faith, hope and love — and the greatest of these is love." (1 Corinthians 13:13)

Date:_____

Title of
Entry:_____

_____

Stay on course; stay on track; never lose courage; never lose hope. Do not permit racism to distract you from your course and God's purpose for your life. Have the audacity to believe that positive change is always possible and you are that change—you have the power of Jesus Christ in you to effect change:

"So do not lose the courage you had in the past, which has a great reward. You must hold on, so you can do what God wants and receive what he has promised." Hebrews 10:35-36 (NCV)

_____

"There are three things that will endure — faith, hope and love — and the greatest of these is love." (1 Corinthians 13:13)

Date:_____

Title of
Entry:_____

_____

To be a great leader you must first be a great servant. Jesus Christ served others while He was on earth; then He died for all humanity—He was and still is the greatest Servant and Leader:

"But it should not be that way among you. Whoever wants to become great among you must serve the rest of you like a servant. Whoever wants to become the first among you must serve all of you like a slave." Mark 10:43-44 (NCV)

_____

"There are three things that will endure — faith, hope and love — and the greatest of these is love." (1 Corinthians 13:13)

Date:_____

Title of
Entry:_____

_____

To be a great leader you must emerge from great servitude. A great leader believes in the power of God in him to do great things for ordinary people. A great leader receives God's grace and blessings to do greater works through Jesus Christ, His holy Grace to us:

"Most assuredly, I say to you, he who believes in Me, the works that I do he will do also; and greater works than these he will do, because I go to My Father." John 14:12 *"And God can give you more blessings than you need. Then you will always have plenty of everything—enough to give to every good work."* 2 Corinthians 9:8 (NCV)

_____

"There are three things that will endure — faith, hope and love — and the greatest of these is love." (1 Corinthians 13:13)

Date:_____

Title of
Entry:_____

_____

To be a great leader your strength must rely on the power of God within you; so when you are weak, God's strength shows forth through you:

"And He said to me, "My grace is sufficient for you, for My strength is made perfect in weakness." Therefore most gladly I will rather boast in my infirmities, that the power of Christ may rest upon me." (2 Corinthians 12:9)

_____

"There are three things that will endure — faith, hope and love — and the greatest of these is love." (1 Corinthians 13:13)

Date:_____

Title of
Entry:_____

_____

A great leader does not rely on his strength, but rather on God for his or her strength:

"We are not saying that we can do this work ourselves. It is God who makes us able to do all that we do." 2 Corinthians 3:5 (NCV)

_____

"There are three things that will endure — faith, hope and love — and the greatest of these is love." (1 Corinthians 13:13)

Date:_____

Title of Entry:_____

_____

A great leader inspires unity among people of all races or ethnicities:

"In Christ, there is no difference between Jew and Greek, slave and free person, male and female. You are all the same in Christ Jesus." Galatians 3:28 (NCV)

_____

"There are three things that will endure — faith, hope and love — and the greatest of these is love." (1 Corinthians 13:13)

Date:_____

Title of Entry:_____

_____

You must believe that all things are possible through God for you when you believe in Him:

"Jesus said to him, "If you can believe, all things are possible to him who believes." Matthew 13:32 (NKJV)

_____

"There are three things that will endure — faith, hope and love — and the greatest of these is love." (1 Corinthians 13:13)

Date:_____

Title of
Entry:_____

_____

The spirit of fear is a weapon of defeat and destruction, and bondage of the mind. The spirit of fear is not of God:

"For the Spirit God gave us does not make us timid, but gives us power, love and self-discipline." 2 Timothy 1:7 (NKJV)

_____

"There are three things that will endure — faith, hope and love — and the greatest of these is love." (1 Corinthians 13:13)

Date:_____

Title of Entry:_____

_____

Do not be anxious about the works and actions of those who perpetrate and perpetuate evil against us, because their activities are only temporary:

"Do not fret because of those who are evil or be envious of those who do wrong; for like the grass they will soon wither, like green plants they will soon die away." Psalms 37:1-2 (NKJV)

_____

"There are three things that will endure — faith, hope and love — and the greatest of these is love." (1 Corinthians 13:13)

Date:_____

Title of
Entry:_____

_____

You must never allow the fear of anything to take root within your soul except the fear of God, which are love, reverence and utmost respect of God Almighty:

"The fear of man brings a snare, but whoever trusts in the Lord shall be safe." Proverbs 29:25 (NKJV)

_____

"There are three things that will endure — faith, hope and love — and the greatest of these is love." (1 Corinthians 13:13)

Date:_____

Title of
Entry:_____

_____

You should not accept racism or any unjust or oppressive action against you based on your carnal fear, but rather you should choose God's path of justice, and believe and trust God's Holy Word for victory over any form of injustice and inequity:

"For God has not given us a spirit of fear, but of power and of love and of a sound mind." 2 Timothy 1:7 (NKJV)

_____

"There are three things that will endure — faith, hope and love — and the greatest of these is love." (1 Corinthians 13:13)

Date:_____

Title of
Entry:_____

_____

By faith, a spiritual fight that is sustained by God's supernatural power in you through Jesus Christ, is greater than evils such as racism, and will open up His paths of justice and provide you physical strategies to deal with and overcome racism:

"Behold, all those who were incensed against you shall be ashamed and disgraced; they shall be as nothing, and those who strive with you shall perish. You shall seek them and not find them —those who contended with you. Those who war against you shall be as nothing, as a nonexistent thing. For I, the LORD your God, will hold your right hand, saying to you, 'Fear not, I will help you.'" Isaiah 41:11-13 (NKJV)

_____

Date:_____

Title of
Entry:_____

_____

The good news is that God can turn racist actions designed to cause unfavorable effects against us into favorable consequences:

"And we know that all things work together for good to those who love God, to those who are the called according to His purpose." Romans 8:28 (NKJV)

_____

Date:_____

Title of Entry:_____

_____

Let your heart, mind, thoughts and words reflect your utmost confidence in God. In prayer and thanksgiving, make your requests to God:

"Plead my cause, O Lord, with those who strive against me; fight against those who fight against me. Take hold of my shield and buckler and stand up for my help. Also draw out the spear, and stop those who pursue me. Say to my soul, 'I am your salvation.'" Psalms 35:1-3 (NKJV)

_____

"There are three things that will endure — faith, hope and love — and the greatest of these is love." (1 Corinthians 13:13)

Date:_____

Title of
Entry:_____

_____

The real victory over fear of anything, including fear of racism, is never the complete absence of fear in our lives, but the permanent presence of our Christ-rooted courage that constantly resists and dispels fear, leaving no room for it to have prolonged or permanent residence within our soul:

"Be strong and of good courage, do not be afraid of them; for the Lord your God, He is the One who goes with you. He will not leave you nor forsake you." Deuteronomy 31:6 (NKJV) *"Be of good courage, And He shall strengthen your heart, all you who hope in the Lord."* Psalms 31:24 (NKJV)

_____

"There are three things that will endure — faith, hope and love — and the greatest of these is love." (1 Corinthians 13:13)

Date:_____

Title of
Entry:_____

_____

You must not fear the evil spirit of racism. You should not fear the dark powers of the abhorrent spirit of racism. You must not fear the words and actions of racists, for you are a child of God through Jesus Christ, the Seed of Abraham; therefore, you are a child of God's promises—a child of God's victory through the precious Blood of Jesus Christ:

"Now to Abraham and his Seed were the promises made. He does not say, "And to seeds," as of many, but as of one, "And to your Seed," who is Christ." Galatians 3:16 (NKJV) *"because everyone who is a child of God conquers the world. And this is the victory that conquers the world—our faith."* 1 John 5:4 (NCV)

_____

Date:_____

Title of
Entry:_____

_____

Faith and trust in God gives rise to spiritual courage and wisdom, and banishes all carnal fears. So reverence God and not any mortal man or woman:

"The fear of the Lord is clean, enduring forever; the judgments of the Lord are true and righteous altogether." Psalms 19:9 (NKJV)
"The fear of the Lord leads to life, and he who has it will abide in satisfaction; He will not be visited with evil." Proverbs 19:23 (NKJV)

_____

"There are three things that will endure — faith, hope and love — and the greatest of these is love." (1 Corinthians 13:13)

Date:_____

Title of Entry:_____

_____

God has the power to protect you from the odious spirit of racism and racists. He has the power to remove racist elements from your path. He alone has the authority to absolve your racist attackers and offenders of their actions if they repent and turn from their racist ways or bring them to quick and impartial justice if they fail to repent. God is a pure and holy God who judges and hands out impartial justice, giving equal time for all to repent and change from their wicked ways:

"For the Lord your God is God of gods and Lord of lords, the great God, mighty and awesome, who shows no partiality nor takes a bribe." Deuteronomy 10:17 (NKJV

_____

"There are three things that will endure — faith, hope and love — and the greatest of these is love." (1 Corinthians 13:13)

Date:_____

Title of
Entry:_____

_____

The Sword of the Spirit, God's Word fueled by His Holy Spirit can never and will never fail. God will not relent until every unrepentant racist offender who has attacked you, His anointed vessel, is defeated and brought to His justice:

"For I, the Lord your God, will hold your right hand, saying to you, 'Fear not, I will help you.'" Isaiah 41:13 (NKJV) *"But the Lord your God will deliver them over to you, and will inflict defeat upon them until they are destroyed."* Deuteronomy 7:23 (NKJV)

_____

"There are three things that will endure — faith, hope and love — and the greatest of these is love." (1 Corinthians 13:13)

Date:_____

Title of Entry:_____

_____

Racism and its evils can cause us deep wounds and hurts within our soul, and to forgive our racist offenders, which we must, we need God's enabling grace to successfully accomplish this without holding onto any unforgiveness:

"For the Lord God is a sun and shield; the Lord will give grace and glory; no good thing will He withhold from those who walk uprightly." Psalms 84:11 (NKJV) *"But to each one of us grace was given according to the measure of Christ's gift."* Ephesians 4:7 (NKJV) *"Do not judge, and you will not be judged. Do not condemn, and you will not be condemned. Forgive, and you will be forgiven."* Luke 6:47(NIV)

_____

"There are three things that will endure — faith, hope and love — and the greatest of these is love." (1 Corinthians 13:13)

Date:_____

Title of
Entry:_____

_____

Forgive your racist offenders. God has asked us to forgive those who offend us as He forgives us our own offenses. The spiritual consequence of not forgiving our offenders is not receiving forgiveness for our own offenses:

"For if you forgive men their trespasses, your Heavenly Father will also forgive you. But if you do not forgive men their trespasses, neither will your Father forgive your trespasses." Matthew 6:14-15 (NKJV) *"...Forgive and you will be forgiven..."* Luke 6:37 (NKJV)

_____

"There are three things that will endure — faith, hope and love — and the greatest of these is love." (1 Corinthians 13:13)

Date:_____

Title of
Entry:_____

_____

The odious spirit of racism is so evil, manipulative and destructive that we do need godly wisdom and understanding to be able to cope and deal with it and gain spiritual and material triumph over it. If we humble ourselves before God, He will guide and teach us His way of justice, mercy and truth. Through His Son Jesus Christ, our Lord and Savior, He has given us victory over the malicious spirit of racism:

"The humble He guides in justice, and the humble He teaches His way. All the paths of the Lord are mercy and truth..." Psalms 25:9-10 (NKJV) *"For the Lord gives wisdom; from His mouth come knowledge and understanding..."* Proverbs 2:6 (NKJV) *"Understanding is a wellspring of life to him who has it."* Proverbs 16: 22 (NKJV)

_____

Date:_____

Title of Entry:_____

_____

Rather than feel or think like a victim of racism, act more like a conqueror over it through Jesus Christ, Who strengthens you daily, and Who has given you victory it. Have complete confidence in God and say to Him:

"I have confidence in you, in the Lord, that you will have no other mind; but he who troubles you shall bear his judgment whoever he is." Galatians 5:10 (NKJV) *"No, in all these things we are more than conquerors through him who loved us."* Romans 8:37 (NIV)

_____

"There are three things that will endure — faith, hope and love — and the greatest of these is love." (1 Corinthians 13:13)

Date:_____

Title of Entry:_____

_____

As Jesus Christ cried out to God our Father on the Cross, you can do the same when racism weighs down on your soul:

"You know my reproach, my shame and my dishonor; my adversaries are all before You. Reproach has broken my heart and I am full of heaviness; I looked for someone to take pity, but there was none; and for comforters, but I found none. They gave me gall for food, and for my thirst they gave me vinegar to drink." Psalms 69:19-21 (NKJV)

_____

"There are three things that will endure —faith, hope and love — and the greatest of these is love." (1 Corinthians 13:13)

Date:_____

Title of
Entry:_____

_____

Don't allow the loathsome spirit of racism to discourage you. Don't allow the devil to successfully wage a battle against your own mind. You have the power of God's Word against racism. You have the power of God's full armor against racism. You can stand in the glorious victory that Jesus Christ gained for you over evil such as racism:

"Finally, my brethren, be strong in the Lord and in the power of His might. Put on the whole armor of God that you may be able to stand against the wiles of the devil." Ephesians 6:10-11 (NKJV)

_____

"There are three things that will endure — faith, hope and love — and the greatest of these is love." (1 Corinthians 13:13)

Inspirational Quotes

"I have been driven many times to my knees by the overwhelming conviction that I had nowhere else to go. My own wisdom, and that of all about me, seemed insufficient for the day."

President Abraham Lincoln

"In moods of discouragement or despair, never forget that the sunshine will ultimately come back, that it's absence never is permanent. Hang onto your faith, knowing that soon you will rise into the sunshine again."

Norman Vincent Peale

"Being unwanted, unloved, uncared for, forgotten by everybody, I think that is a much greater hunger, a much greater poverty than the person who has nothing to eat...We must find each other."

Blessed Mother Teresa

"There are three things that will endure — faith, hope and love — and the greatest of these is love." (1 Corinthians 13:13)

Personal Inspiration Entry Notes

"There are three things that will endure — faith, hope and love — and the greatest of these is love." (1 Corinthians 13:13)

Date:_____

Title of
Entry:_____

_____

Make the best of your today for your tomorrow starts today. Every day is your tomorrow:

"Never leave that till tomorrow which you can do today."
Benjamin Franklin

_____

"There are three things that will endure — faith, hope and love — and the greatest of these is love." (1 Corinthians 13:13)

Date:_____

Title of
Entry:_____

_____

Anger can be destructive when its negative energy is not channeled into positive, productive works:

"He who angers you conquers you."
Elizabeth Kenny

_____

"There are three things that will endure — faith, hope and love — and the greatest of these is love." (1 Corinthians 13:13)

Date:_____

Title of
Entry:_____

_____

Unrighteous anger distracts you from your focus and goal:

"The proud man hath no God; the envious man hath no neighbor; the angry man hath not himself."
Joseph Hall

_____

"There are three things that will endure — faith, hope and love — and the greatest of these is love." (1 Corinthians 13:13)

Date:_____

**Title of
Entry:**_____

_____

It is up to you what kind of influence you choose to exert on others:

"There have been meetings of only a moment which have left impressions for life ...for eternity. No one can understand that mysterious thing we call 'influence' ...yet everyone of us continually exerts influence, either to heal, to bless, to leave marks of beauty; or to wound, to hurt, to poison, to stain other lives."
J.B. Miller

_____

"There are three things that will endure —faith, hope and love —and the greatest of these is love." (1 Corinthians 13:13)

Date:_____

Title of Entry:_____

_____

There is great power in positive thinking and positive action:

"Change your thoughts and you change your world."
Norman Vincent Peale

"There are three things that will endure — faith, hope and love — and the greatest of these is love." (1 Corinthians 13:13)

Date:_____

Title of
Entry:_____

_____

Never give up, no matter what:

"Never to tire, never to grow cold; to be patient, sympathetic, tender; to look for the budding flower and the opening heart; to hope always, like God, to love always-this is duty."
H.E. Amiel

"There are three things that will endure — faith, hope and love — and the greatest of these is love." (1 Corinthians 13:13)

Date:_____

Title of
Entry:_____

_____

Believe in justice and freedom for all and work actively for it:

"Those who deny freedom to others, deserve it not for themselves; and, under a just God, cannot long retain it."
President Abraham Lincoln

Date:_____

Title of
Entry:_____

_____

Live your life in such a positive manner that it validates your words:

As we express our gratitude, we must never forget that the highest appreciation is not to utter words, but to live by them.
President John F. Kennedy

_____

"There are three things that will endure — faith, hope and love — and the greatest of these is love." (1 Corinthians 13:13)

Date:_____

Title of
Entry:_____

_____

Your sense of purpose fuels your strength and courage:

"Efforts and courage are not enough without purpose and direction."
President John F. Kennedy

_____

"There are three things that will endure — faith, hope and love — and the greatest of these is love." (1 Corinthians 13:13)

Date:_____

Title of
Entry:_____

_____

Jesus Christ accomplished in three years of His life what men cannot achieve in decades of a lifetime. God prepared Him for thirty years for His three-year ministry, which every generation will hear about through eternity. Strive for quality years in your life:

"And in the end, it's not the years in your life that count. It's the life in your years."
President Abraham Lincoln

_____

"There are three things that will endure — faith, hope and love — and the greatest of these is love." (1 Corinthians 13:13)

Date:_____

Title of
Entry:_____

_____

Do not be discouraged when you are opposed whilst doing what is right; remain focused and on course:

"Great spirits have always encountered violent opposition from mediocre minds."
Albert Einstein

_____

"There are three things that will endure — faith, hope and love — and the greatest of these is love." (1 Corinthians 13:13)

Date:_____

Title of Entry:_____

_____

Positive thoughts and plans must then be put into strategic action:

"You cannot plough a field by turning it over in your mind."
Author Unknown

_____

"There are three things that will endure — faith, hope and love — and the greatest of these is love." (1 Corinthians 13:13)

Date:_____

Title of
Entry:_____

_____

God's purpose for you should lead and drive your daily focus in order for you to succeed:

"Nothing contributes so much to tranquilize the mind as a steady purpose - a point on which the soul may fix its intellectual eye."
Mary Shelley

_____

"There are three things that will endure — faith, hope and love — and the greatest of these is love." (1 Corinthians 13:13)

Date:_____

Title of
Entry:_____

_____

Fear of failure should never stop you from trying:

"It is hard to fail, but it is worse never to have tried to succeed."
President Theodore Roosevelt
_____

"There are three things that will endure — faith, hope and love — and the greatest of these is love." (1 Corinthians 13:13)

Date:_____

**Title of
Entry:**_____

_____

Your journey to success must start with you, guided by the awesome power of God:

"Do not wait for leaders; do it alone, person to person."
Blessed Mother Teresa

_____

"There are three things that will endure — faith, hope and love — and the greatest of these is love." (1 Corinthians 13:13)

Date:_____

**Title of
Entry:**_____

_____

Faith requires that you take the first step and God will guide you through all the necessary steps:

"God doesn't require us to succeed; he only requires that you try."
Blessed Mother Teresa

_____

"There are three things that will endure — faith, hope and love — and the greatest of these is love." (1 Corinthians 13:13)

Date:_____

Title of
Entry:_____

_____

Be faithful in all that you do and success will follow:

"I do not pray for success, I ask for faithfulness."
Blessed Mother Teresa

_____

"There are three things that will endure — faith, hope and love — and the greatest of these is love." (1 Corinthians 13:13)

Date: _____

Title of Entry: _____

_____

Remember to take time to pray; to worship and praise God; to spend quality time in solitude with God; for it is in quietness that God pours out His Heart to us and delivers His purpose for our lives:

"We need to find God, and He cannot be found in noise and restlessness. God is the friend of silence. See how nature—trees, flowers, grass- grows in silence; see the stars, the moon and the sun, how they move in silence... We need silence to be able to touch souls. "
Blessed Mother Teresa

_____

"There are three things that will endure — faith, hope and love — and the greatest of these is love." (1 Corinthians 13:13)

Date:_____

Title of
Entry:_____

_____

You must never be afraid to be motivated to change or for change. You must never be afraid to take the first step for positive change. You must never be hesitant to join the motivated to effect positive change:

"Progress is a nice word. But change is its motivator. And change has its enemies. "
Senator Robert F. Kennedy
_____

Date:_____

Title of
Entry:_____

_____

Reject and resist racism in whatever you do because racism is a quiet destroyer of the human soul:

"I detest racialism, because I regard it as a barbaric thing, whether it comes from a black man or a white man."
President Nelson Mandela

_____

"There are three things that will endure — faith, hope and love — and the greatest of these is love." (1 Corinthians 13:13)

Personal Revelation Entry Notes

Write down God's Revelation to you, His spoken word to you (Rhema) or other thoughts and ideas that come spontaneously to you.

"Rhema" is a word of revelation, prophecy, or knowledge, through the mouth of God, personally spoken to you or deposited in your heart, in regards to a particular circumstance, situation or problem.

When God gives you a vision, hold it dear to your heart; work hard to achieve it; trust and never doubt Him.

"For the vision is yet for an appointed time, but at the end it shall speak, and not lie: though it tarry, wait for it; because it will surely come, it will not tarry."
Habakkuk 2:3 (NKJV)

"There are three things that will endure — faith, hope and love — and the greatest of these is love." (1 Corinthians 13:13)

Date: _____

Theme/Topic/Focus: _____

_____

Business Ideas: _____

"There are three things that will endure — faith, hope and love — and the greatest of these is love." (1 Corinthians 13:13)

Other Ideas/Thoughts: _____

"There are three things that will endure — faith, hope and love — and the greatest of these is love." (1 Corinthians 13:13)

My Rays of Victory Bible Study Diary

Date: _____

Theme/Topic/Focus: _____

_____

Business

Ideas: _____

"There are three things that will endure — faith, hope and love — and the greatest of these is love." (1 Corinthians 13:13)

Other Ideas/Thoughts: _____

"There are three things that will endure —faith, hope and love —and the greatest of these is love." (1 Corinthians 13:13)

Date: _____

Theme/Topic/Focus: _____

_____

Business Ideas: _____

"There are three things that will endure — faith, hope and love — and the greatest of these is love." (1 Corinthians 13:13)

Other Ideas/Thoughts: _____

"There are three things that will endure — faith, hope and love — and the greatest of these is love." (1 Corinthians 13:13)

My Rays of Victory Bible Study Diary

Date: _____

Theme/Topic/Focus: _____

_____

Business

Ideas: _____

"There are three things that will endure — faith, hope and love — and the greatest of these is love." (1 Corinthians 13:13)

Other Ideas/Thoughts: _____

"There are three things that will endure — faith, hope and love — and the greatest of these is love." (1 Corinthians 13:13)

Date: _____

Theme/Topic/Focus: _____

_____

Business Ideas: _____

"There are three things that will endure — faith, hope and love — and the greatest of these is love." (1 Corinthians 13:13)

Other Ideas/Thoughts:_____

"There are three things that will endure — faith, hope and love — and the greatest of these is love." (1 Corinthians 13:13)

Date: _____

Theme/Topic/Focus:_____

_____

Business

Ideas:_____

"There are three things that will endure — faith, hope and love — and the greatest of these is love." (1 Corinthians 13:13)

Other Ideas/Thoughts: _____

"There are three things that will endure — faith, hope and love — and the greatest of these is love." (1 Corinthians 13:13)

Date: _____

Theme/Topic/Focus: _____

_____

Business

Ideas: _____

"There are three things that will endure — faith, hope and love — and the greatest of these is love." (1 Corinthians 13:13)

Other Ideas/Thoughts: _____

"There are three things that will endure — faith, hope and love — and the greatest of these is love." (1 Corinthians 13:13)

Date: _____

Theme/Topic/Focus: _____

_____

Business Ideas: _____

"There are three things that will endure — faith, hope and love — and the greatest of these is love." (1 Corinthians 13:13)

Other Ideas/Thoughts: _____

"There are three things that will endure — faith, hope and love — and the greatest of these is love." (1 Corinthians 13:13)

Date: _____

Theme/Topic/Focus:_____

_____

Business
Ideas:_____

"There are three things that will endure — faith, hope and love — and the greatest of these is love." (1 Corinthians 13:13)

Other Ideas/Thoughts: _____

"There are three things that will endure — faith, hope and love — and the greatest of these is love." (1 Corinthians 13:13)

Date: _____

Theme/Topic/Focus: _____

_____

Business Ideas: _____

"There are three things that will endure — faith, hope and love — and the greatest of these is love." (1 Corinthians 13:13)

Other Ideas/Thoughts:_____

"There are three things that will endure — faith, hope and love — and the greatest of these is love." (1 Corinthians 13:13)

My Rays of Victory Bible Study Diary

Date: _____

Theme/Topic/Focus: _____

_____

Business Ideas: _____

"There are three things that will endure — faith, hope and love — and the greatest of these is love." (1 Corinthians 13:13)

Other Ideas/Thoughts:_____

"There are three things that will endure — faith, hope and love — and the greatest of these is love." (1 Corinthians 13:13)

My Rays of Victory Bible Study Diary

Date: _____

Theme/Topic/Focus:_____

_____

Business
Ideas:_____

My Rays of Victory Bible Study Diary

"There are three things that will endure — faith, hope and love — and the greatest of these is love." (1 Corinthians 13:13)

Other Ideas/Thoughts: _____

"There are three things that will endure — faith, hope and love — and the greatest of these is love." *(1 Corinthians 13:13)*

My Rays of Victory Bible Study Diary

Date: _____

Theme/Topic/Focus: _____

_____

Business

Ideas: _____

"There are three things that will endure — faith, hope and love — and the greatest of these is love." (1 Corinthians 13:13)

Other Ideas/Thoughts: _____

"There are three things that will endure — faith, hope and love — and the greatest of these is love." (1 Corinthians 13:13)

My Rays of Victory Bible Study Diary

Date: _____

Theme/Topic/Focus:_____

_____

Business

Ideas:_____

"There are three things that will endure — faith, hope and love — and the greatest of these is love." (1 Corinthians 13:13)

Other Ideas/Thoughts: _____

"There are three things that will endure — faith, hope and love — and the greatest of these is love." (1 Corinthians 13:13)

Date: _____

Theme/Topic/Focus:_____

_____

Business
Ideas:_____

"There are three things that will endure — faith, hope and love — and the greatest of these is love." (1 Corinthians 13:13)

Other Ideas/Thoughts: _____

"There are three things that will endure — faith, hope and love — and the greatest of these is love." (1 Corinthians 13:13)

Bible Reading Schedule

[Month (Heading)/Day/Bible Chapter/Bible Verse(s)]

This Bible Reading Schedule is courtesy of www.thebible.net.

JANUARY	FEBRUARY	MARCH
1 Genesis 1-3	1 Leviticus 1-4	1 Deuter. 5-7
2 Genesis 4-7	2 Leviticus 5-7	2 Deuter. 8-10
3 Genesis 8-11	3 Leviticus 8-9	3 Deuter. 11-13
4 Genesis 12-15	4 Leviticus 10-12	4 Deuter. 14-17
5 Genesis 16-18	5 Leviticus 13	5 Deuter. 18-20
6 Genesis 19-20	6 Leviticus 14-15	6 Deuter. 21-23
7 Genesis 21-23	7 Leviticus 16-18	7 Deuter. 24-26
8 Genesis 24-25	8 Leviticus 19-21	8 Deuter. 27-28
9 Genesis 26-28	9 Leviticus 22-23	9 Deuter. 29-31
10 Genesis 29-30	10 Leviticus 24-25	10 Deuter. 32-34
11 Genesis 31-32	11 Leviticus 26-27	11 Joshua 1-4
12 Genesis 33-35	12 Numbers 1-2	12 Joshua 5-7
13 Genesis 36-38	13 Numbers 3-4	13 Joshua 8-9
14 Genesis 39-41	14 Numbers 5-6	14 Joshua 10-11
15 Genesis 42-44	15 Numbers 7	15 Joshua 12-14
16 Genesis 45-47	16 Numbers 8-10	16 Joshua 15-17
17 Genesis 48-50	17 Numbers 11-13	17 Joshua 18-20
18 Exodus 1-3	18 Numbers 14-15	18 Joshua 21-22
19 Exodus 4-6	19 Numbers 16-18	19 Joshua 23-24
20 Exodus 7-9	20 Numbers 19-21	20 Judges 1-3
21 Exodus 10-12	21 Numbers 22-24	21 Judges 4-6
22 Exodus 13-15	22 Numbers 25-26	22 Judges 7-8
23 Exodus 16-18	23 Numbers 27-29	23 Judges 9-10

"There are three things that will endure — faith, hope and love — and the greatest of these is love." (1 Corinthians 13:13)

24 Exodus 19-21	24 Numbers 30-31	24 Judges 11-13
25 Exodus 22-24	25 Numbers 32-33	25 Judges 14-16
26 Exodus 25-27	26 Numbers 34-36	26 Judges 17-19
27 Exodus 28-29	27 Deuter. 1-2	27 Judges 20-21
28 Exodus 30-32	28 Deuter. 3-4	28 Ruth 1-4
29 Exodus 33-35		29 1 Samuel 1-3
30 Exodus 36-38	**MAY**	30 1 Samuel 4-7
31 Exodus 39-40	1 2 Kings 8-9	31 1 Samuel 8-10
	2 2 Kings 10-12	
APRIL	3 2 Kings 13-14	**JUNE**
1 1 Samuel 11-13	4 2 Kings 15-16	1 Ezra 9-10
2 1 Samuel 14-15	5 2 Kings 17-18	2 Nehemiah 1-3
3 1 Samuel 16-17	6 2 Kings 19-21	3 Nehemiah 4-6
4 1 Samuel 18-20	7 2 Kings 22-25	4 Nehemiah 7-8
5 1 Samuel 21-24	8 1 Chron. 1	5 Nehemiah 9-10
6 1 Samuel 25-27	9 1 Chron. 2-4	6 Nehemiah 11-13
7 1 Samuel 28-31	10 1 Chron. 5-6	7 Esther 1-3
8 2 Samuel 1-3	11 1 Chron. 7-9	8 Esther 4-7
9 2 Samuel 4-7	12 1 Chron. 10-12	9 Esther 8-10
10 2 Samuel 8-11	13 1 Chron. 13-16	10 Job 1-5
11 2 Samuel 12-13	14 1 Chron. 17-19	11 Job 6-10
12 2 Samuel 14-15	15 1 Chron. 20-23	12 Job 11-15
13 2 Samuel 16-17	16 1 Chron. 24-26	13 Job 16-21
14 2 Samuel 18-19	17 1 Chron. 27-29	14 Job 22-28
15 2 Samuel 20-22	18 2 Chron. 1-4	15 Job 29-33
16 2 Samuel 23-24	19 2 Chron. 5-7	16 Job 34-37
17 1 Kings 1	20 2 Chron. 8-10	17 Job 38-42
18 1 Kings 2-3	21 2 Chron. 11-14	18 Psalms 1-9
19 1 Kings 4-6	22 2 Chron. 15-18	19 Psalms 10-17
20 1 Kings 7	23 2 Chron. 19-22	20 Psalms 18-22
21 1 Kings 8	24 2 Chron. 23-25	21 Psalms 23-31
22 1 Kings 9-10	25 2 Chron. 26-28	22 Psalms 32-37
23 1 Kings 11-12	26 2 Chron. 29-30	23 Psalms 38-44
24 1 Kings 13-14	27 2 Chron. 31-33	24 Psalms 45-51
25 1 Kings 15-17	28 2 Chron. 34-36	25 Psalms 52-59
26 1 Kings 18-19	29 Ezra 1-2	26 Psalms 60-67
27 1 Kings 20-22	30 Ezra 3-5	27 Psalms 68-71
28 2 Kings 1-2	31 Ezra 6-8	28 Psalms 72-77

"There are three things that will endure — faith, hope and love — and the greatest of these is love." (1 Corinthians 13:13)

29 2 Kings 3-4 30 2 Kings 5-7 **JULY** 1 Psalms 90-97 2 Psalms 98-104 3 Psalms 105-107 4 Psalms 108-116 5 Psalms 117-118 6 Psalms 119 7 Psalms 120-135 8 Psalms 136-142 9 Psalms 143-150 10 Proverbs 1-4 11 Proverbs 5-8 12 Proverbs 9-13 13 Proverbs 14-17 14 Proverbs 18-21 15 Proverbs 22-24 16 Proverbs 25-28 17 Proverbs 29-31 18 Eccles. 1-6 19 Eccles. 7-12 20 Song of Sol 1-8 21 Isaiah 1-4 22 Isaiah 5-8 23 Isaiah 9-12 24 Isaiah 13-16 25 Isaiah 17-21 26 Isaiah 22-25 27 Isaiah 26-28 28 Isaiah 29-31 29 Isaiah 32-35 30 Isaiah 36-38 31 Isaiah 39-42	**AUGUST** 1 Isaiah 43-47 2 Isaiah 48-51 3 Isaiah 52-56 4 Isaiah 57-59 5 Isaiah 60-63 6 Isaiah 64-66 7 Jeremiah 1-3 8 Jeremiah 4-6 9 Jeremiah 7-9 10 Jeremiah 10-12 11 Jeremiah 13-15 12 Jeremiah 16-18 13 Jeremiah 19-22 14 Jeremiah 23-25 15 Jeremiah 26-27 16 Jeremiah 28-30 17 Jeremiah 31-32 18 Jeremiah 33-35 19 Jeremiah 36-38 20 Jeremiah 39-41 21 Jeremiah 42-44 22 Jeremiah 45-48 23 Jeremiah 49-50 24 Jeremiah 51-52 25 Lamentations 1-2 26 Lamentations 3-5 27 Ezekiel 1-4 28 Ezekiel 5-8 29 Ezekiel 9-12 30 Ezekiel 13-15 31 Ezekiel 16	29 Psalms 78-81 30 Psalms 82-89 **SEPTEMBER** 1 Ezekiel 17-19 2 Ezekiel 20-21 3 Ezekiel 22-23 4 Ezekiel 24-26 5 Ezekiel 27-28 6 Ezekiel 29-31 7 Ezekiel 32-33 8 Ezekiel 34-36 9 Ezekiel 37-38 10 Ezekiel 39-40 11 Ezekiel 41-43 12 Ezekiel 44-45 13 Ezekiel 46-48 14 Daniel 1-2 15 Daniel 3-4 16 Daniel 5-6 17 Daniel 7-8 18 Daniel 9-10 19 Daniel 11-12 20 Hosea 1-7 21 Hosea 8-14 22 Joel 1-3 23 Amos 1-5 24 Amos 6-9/Obad. 25 Jon.1-4/Mic.1-2 26 Micah 3-7 27 Nahum/Habak. 28 Zeph./Haggai 29 Zechariah 1-6 30 Zechariah 7-10

"There are three things that will endure — faith, hope and love — and the greatest of these is love." (1 Corinthians 13:13)

OCTOBER	NOVEMBER	DECEMBER
1 Zechariah 11-14	1 Luke 21-22	1 1 Corinth.12-14
2 Malachi 1-4	2 Luke 23-24	2 1 Corinth.15-16
3 Matthew 1-4	3 John 1-3	3 2 Corinth. 1-4
4 Matthew 5-6	4 John 4-5	4 2 Corinth. 5-8
5 Matthew 7-9	5 John 6-7	5 2 Corinth. 9-13
6 Matthew 10-12	6 John 8-9	6 Galatians 1-6
7 Matthew 13-14	7 John 10-11	7 Ephesians 1-3
8 Matthew 15-17	8 John 12-13	8 Ephesians 4-6
9 Matthew 18-20	9 John 14-16	9 Philippians 1-4
10 Matthew 21-22	10 John 17-18	10 Colossians 1-4
11 Matthew 23-24	11 John 19-21	11 1 Thess. 1-5
12 Matthew 25-26	12 Acts 1-3	12 2 Thess. 1-3
13 Matthew 27-28	13 Acts 4-6	13 1 Timothy 1-4
14 Mark 1-3	14 Acts 7-8	14 1 Timothy 5-6
15 Mark 4-5	15 Acts 9-10	15 2 Timothy 1-4
16 Mark 6-7	16 Acts 11-13	16 Titus/Philemon
17 Mark 8-9	17 Acts 14-16	17 Hebrews 1-5
18 Mark 10-11	18 Acts 17-18	18 Hebrews 6-9
19 Mark 12-13	19 Acts 19-20	19 Hebrews 10-11
20 Mark 14-16	20 Acts 21-22	20 Hebrews 12-13
21 Luke 1	21 Acts 23-25	21 James 1-5
22 Luke 2-3	22 Acts 26-28	22 1 Peter 1-5
23 Luke 4-5	23 Romans 1-3	23 2 Peter 1-3
24 Luke 6-7	24 Romans 4-7	24 1 John 1-5
25 Luke 8	25 Romans 8-10	25 2, 3 John, Jude
26 Luke 9	26 Romans 11-14	26 Revelation 1-3
27 Luke 10-11	27 Romans 15-16	27 Revelation 4-8
28 Luke 12-13	28 1 Corinth. 1-4	28 Revelation 9-12
29 Luke 14-16	29 1 Corinth. 5-8	29 Revelation 13-16
30 Luke 17-18	30 1 Corinth. 9-11	30 Revelation 17-19
31 Luke 19-20		31 Revelation 20-22

The above Bible Reading Schedule is from www.thebible.net.

"There are three things that will endure — faith, hope and love — and the greatest of these is love." (1 Corinthians 13:13)

Bible Study Entry Notes

"There are three things that will endure — faith, hope and love — and the greatest of these is love." (1 Corinthians 13:13)

Date:_____ **Bible Theme:**_____

Scripture Study:_____

Main Focus:_____

"There are three things that will endure — faith, hope and love — and the greatest of these is love." (1 Corinthians 13:13)

Date:_____ **Bible Theme:**_____

Scripture Study:_____

Main Focus:_____

"There are three things that will endure — faith, hope and love — and the greatest of these is love." (1 Corinthians 13:13)

Date:_____ Bible Theme:_____

Scripture Study:_____

Main Focus:_____

"There are three things that will endure — faith, hope and love — and the greatest of these is love." (1 Corinthians 13:13)

Date:_____ **Bible Theme:**_____

Scripture Study:_____

Main Focus:_____

"There are three things that will endure — faith, hope and love — and the greatest of these is love." (1 Corinthians 13:13)

Date:_____ Bible Theme:_____

Scripture Study:_____

Main Focus:_____

"There are three things that will endure — faith, hope and love — and the greatest of these is love." (1 Corinthians 13:13)

Date:_____ **Bible Theme:**_____

Scripture Study:_____

Main Focus:_____

"There are three things that will endure — faith, hope and love — and the greatest of these is love." (1 Corinthians 13:13)

Date:_____ **Bible Theme:**_____

Scripture Study:_____

Main Focus:_____

"There are three things that will endure — faith, hope and love — and the greatest of these is love." (1 Corinthians 13:13)

Date:_____ **Bible Theme:**_____

Scripture Study:_____

Main Focus:_____

"There are three things that will endure — faith, hope and love — and the greatest of these is love." (1 Corinthians 13:13)

Date:_____ **Bible Theme:**_____

Scripture Study:_____

Main Focus:_____

"There are three things that will endure — faith, hope and love — and the greatest of these is love." (1 Corinthians 13:13)

Date:_____ **Bible Theme:**_____

Scripture Study:_____

Main Focus:_____

"There are three things that will endure — faith, hope and love — and the greatest of these is love." (1 Corinthians 13:13)

Date:_____ Bible Theme:_____

Scripture Study:_____

Main Focus:_____

"There are three things that will endure — faith, hope and love — and the greatest of these is love." (1 Corinthians 13:13)

Date:_____ **Bible Theme:**_____

Scripture Study:_____

Main Focus:_____

"There are three things that will endure — faith, hope and love — and the greatest of these is love." (1 Corinthians 13:13)

Date:_____ **Bible Theme:**_____

Scripture Study:_____

Main Focus:_____

"There are three things that will endure — faith, hope and love — and the greatest of these is love." (1 Corinthians 13:13)

Date:_____ **Bible Theme:**_____

Scripture Study:_____

Main Focus:_____

"There are three things that will endure — faith, hope and love — and the greatest of these is love." (1 Corinthians 13:13)

Date:_____ **Bible Theme:**_____

Scripture Study:_____

Main Focus:_____

"There are three things that will endure — faith, hope and love — and the greatest of these is love." (1 Corinthians 13:13)

Date:_____ **Bible Theme:**_____

Scripture Study:_____

Main Focus:_____

"There are three things that will endure — faith, hope and love — and the greatest of these is love." (1 Corinthians 13:13)

Date:_____ **Bible Theme:**_____

Scripture Study:_____

Main Focus:_____

"There are three things that will endure — faith, hope and love — and the greatest of these is love." (1 Corinthians 13:13)

Date:_____ **Bible Theme:**_____

Scripture Study:_____

Main Focus:_____

"There are three things that will endure — faith, hope and love — and the greatest of these is love." (1 Corinthians 13:13)

General Notes

"There are three things that will endure — faith, hope and love — and the greatest of these is love." (1 Corinthians 13:13)

Date:_____ **Topic:**_____

_____

"There are three things that will endure — faith, hope and love — and the greatest of these is love." (1 Corinthians 13:13)

Date:_____ **Topic:**_____

_____

"There are three things that will endure — faith, hope and love — and the greatest of these is love." (1 Corinthians 13:13)

Date:_____ **Topic:**_____

_____

"There are three things that will endure — faith, hope and love — and the greatest of these is love." (1 Corinthians 13:13)

Date:_____ Topic:_____

_____

"There are three things that will endure — faith, hope and love — and the greatest of these is love." (1 Corinthians 13:13)

Date:_____ Topic:_____

_____

"There are three things that will endure — faith, hope and love — and the greatest of these is love." (1 Corinthians 13:13)

Date:_____ **Topic:**_____

_____

"There are three things that will endure — faith, hope and love — and the greatest of these is love." (1 Corinthians 13:13)

Date:_____ **Topic:**_____

_____

"There are three things that will endure —faith, hope and love —and the greatest of these is love." (1 Corinthians 13:13)

Date:_____ **Topic:**_____

_____

"There are three things that will endure — faith, hope and love — and the greatest of these is love." (1 Corinthians 13:13)

Date:_____**Topic:**_____

_____

"There are three things that will endure — faith, hope and love — and the greatest of these is love." (1 Corinthians 13:13)

Date:_____**Topic:**_____

_____

"There are three things that will endure — faith, hope and love — and the greatest of these is love." (1 Corinthians 13:13)

Date:_____ Topic:_____

_____

"There are three things that will endure — faith, hope and love — and the greatest of these is love." (1 Corinthians 13:13)

Date:_____ **Topic:**_____

_____

"There are three things that will endure — faith, hope and love — and the greatest of these is love." (1 Corinthians 13:13)

Date:_____ **Topic:**_____

_____

"There are three things that will endure — faith, hope and love — and the greatest of these is love." (1 Corinthians 13:13)

Date:_____ **Topic:**_____

_____

"There are three things that will endure — faith, hope and love — and the greatest of these is love." (1 Corinthians 13:13)

Date:_____**Topic:**_____

_____

"There are three things that will endure — faith, hope and love — and the greatest of these is love." (1 Corinthians 13:13)

Date:_____ **Topic:**_____

_____

"There are three things that will endure — faith, hope and love — and the greatest of these is love." (1 Corinthians 13:13)

Date:_____ **Topic:**_____

_____

"There are three things that will endure — faith, hope and love — and the greatest of these is love." (1 Corinthians 13:13)

Date:_____ **Topic:**_____

_____

"There are three things that will endure —faith, hope and love —and the greatest of these is love." (1 Corinthians 13:13)

Date:_____ **Topic:**_____

_____

"There are three things that will endure — faith, hope and love — and the greatest of these is love." (1 Corinthians 13:13)

Date:_____ **Topic:**_____

_____

"There are three things that will endure — faith, hope and love — and the greatest of these is love." (1 Corinthians 13:13)

Date:_____ **Topic:**_____

_____

"There are three things that will endure — faith, hope and love — and the greatest of these is love." (1 Corinthians 13:13)

Date:_____ Topic:_____

_____

"There are three things that will endure — faith, hope and love — and the greatest of these is love." (1 Corinthians 13:13)

Date:_____**Topic:**_____

_____

"There are three things that will endure — faith, hope and love — and the greatest of these is love." (1 Corinthians 13:13)

Date:_____ Topic:_____

_____

"There are three things that will endure — faith, hope and love — and the greatest of these is love." (1 Corinthians 13:13)

Date:_____ **Topic:**_____

_____

"There are three things that will endure — faith, hope and love — and the greatest of these is love." (1 Corinthians 13:13)

Date:_____ **Topic:**_____

_____

"There are three things that will endure —faith, hope and love —and the greatest of these is love." (1 Corinthians 13:13)

Date:_____ Topic:_____

_____

"There are three things that will endure — faith, hope and love — and the greatest of these is love." (1 Corinthians 13:13)

Date:_____ Topic:_____

_____

"There are three things that will endure —faith, hope and love — and the greatest of these is love." (1 Corinthians 13:13)

Date:_____ Topic:_____

_____

"There are three things that will endure — faith, hope and love — and the greatest of these is love." (1 Corinthians 13:13)

Power Thoughts Against Racism

(Excerpts from "Nailing Racism to the Cross")

Your racial and ethnic makeup is made in God's Excellent Image.

*****

The whole entity of "you" encompasses your spirit, body and soul, which were created by God.

*****

God's divine favor within you is enough for your spiritual and material success, because He has already blessed you with spiritual gifts, talents and great potential.

*****

God has given you many million-dollar talents and gifts.

*****

You are a special person with a unique purpose in life.

*****

"There are three things that will endure — faith, hope and love — and the greatest of these is love." (1 Corinthians 13:13)

You are God's deliberate, special and unique creation and you are not a mishap, coincidence, mistake or shame.

*****

You are not illegitimate; Jesus Christ has made you legitimate.

*****

You are a blessing to yourself, your family, your friends, your racist enemies and others, and to the world.

*****

The actions of a prejudiced or racist person lack the ultimate power to stop you from achieving your success, unless you allow them.

*****

The real "You" comes from your spirit that has been redeemed through Jesus Christ and empowered by the Holy Spirit of God; and hrough Jesus Christ, the only Mediator, you have access to God.

*****

You were made in the perfect Image of an awesome God, and through Jesus Christ, you have become a child of God.

*****

The Holy Spirit of God helps you to live holy through Jesus Christ, activate your inherent measure of faith, and

"There are three things that will endure — faith, hope and love — and the greatest of these is love." (1 Corinthians 13:13)

drive your creativity (in your soul) through the "super conscious" locus (core) of your spirit.

****

Knowing God through Jesus Christ and understanding your true spiritual nature is the gateway to knowing His purpose for your individual life.

*****

Through Jesus Christ, God has made you larger than racism.

*****

Authentic spiritual knowledge fuels true self-knowledge and is a silent gear that pushes against racism until it is permanently stalled and unable to attack or erode your psyche or soul.

*****

God's Holy Word is true heavenly knowledge that gives you spiritual wisdom for mental resistance against racism and its evils.

*****

Mental resistance is most effective against racism when your heart and mind are fortified by God's Holy Word.

*****

"There are three things that will endure — faith, hope and love — and the greatest of these is love." (1 Corinthians 13:13)

True self-knowledge is deeply founded in the knowledge of God, Who is the Fountain and Source of all true knowledge.

*****

Within your life's journey is your spiritual purpose as God designed for your life.

*****

God's grace is more than sufficient for you to gain individual victory over racism.

*****

You must exercise positive spiritual dominance over racism through spiritual warfare to experience actual victory in your physical environment.

*****

God's spiritual truth and understanding gives you wisdom to deal victoriously with racism.

*****

For the power of God's Holy Word against racism to work on your behalf, you must believe it, embrace it and activate the measure of faith in you.

*****

Racism is no match against the power of God.

*****

"There are three things that will endure — faith, hope and love — and the greatest of these is love." (1 Corinthians 13:13)

The key to the mantle of spiritual victory over racism lies within you.

*****

God has not given you a spirit of fear, but of love, power and a sound mind.

*****

Fear is not of God, but of the devil, the prince of the air and the ruler of this world.

*****

Fear is the devil's weapon that is designed to cripple your faith and hold you under carnal bondage.

*****

The spirit of fear is a weapon of defeat and destruction, and bondage of the mind.

*****

The power of your faith through Jesus Christ activates your spiritual warfare and releases God's invisible and invincible holy army against the loathsome spirit of racism which operates within racists.

*****

The power of your faith through Jesus Christ smothers and suffocates the evil activities of the foul spirit of racism.

"There are three things that will endure — faith, hope and love — and the greatest of these is love." (1 Corinthians 13:13)

Jesus Christ has set you free from fear of racism and racists, and from fear of any kind.

"There are three things that will endure — faith, hope and love — and the greatest of these is love." (1 Corinthians 13:13)

Date:_____

Title of
Entry:_____

_____

My Personal Commitment Against Racism:

"There are three things that will endure — faith, hope and love — and the greatest of these is love." (1 Corinthians 13:13)

Date:_____

Title of
Entry:_____

_____

My Personal Commitment Against Racism:

"There are three things that will endure — faith, hope and love — and the greatest of these is love." (1 Corinthians 13:13)

Date:_____

Title of
Entry:_____

_____

My Personal Commitment Against Racism:

"There are three things that will endure — faith, hope and love — and the greatest of these is love." (1 Corinthians 13:13)

Date:_____

**Title of
Entry:**_____

_____

My Personal Commitment Against Racism:

"There are three things that will endure — faith, hope and love — and the greatest of these is love." (1 Corinthians 13:13)

Date:_____

Title of
Entry:_____

_____

My Personal Commitment Against Racism:

"There are three things that will endure — faith, hope and love — and the greatest of these is love." (1 Corinthians 13:13)

My Rays of Victory Bible Study Diary

Date:_____

Title of
Entry:_____

_____

My Personal Commitment Against Racism:

"There are three things that will endure — faith, hope and love — and the greatest of these is love." (1 Corinthians 13:13)

Date:_____

Title of Entry:_____

_____

My Personal Commitment Against Racism:

"There are three things that will endure — faith, hope and love — and the greatest of these is love." (1 Corinthians 13:13)

Date:_____

**Title of
Entry:**_____

_____

My Personal Commitment Against Racism:

"There are three things that will endure — faith, hope and love — and the greatest of these is love." (1 Corinthians 13:13)

Date:_____

Title of Entry:_____

_____

My Personal Commitment Against Racism:

"There are three things that will endure — faith, hope and love — and the greatest of these is love." (1 Corinthians 13:13)

Date:_____

Title of
Entry:_____

_____

My Personal Commitment Against Racism:

"There are three things that will endure — faith, hope and love — and the greatest of these is love." (1 Corinthians 13:13)

Date:_____

**Title of
Entry:**_____

_____

My Personal Commitment Against Racism:

"There are three things that will endure — faith, hope and love — and the greatest of these is love." (1 Corinthians 13:13)

Date:_____

Title of
Entry:_____

_____

My Personal Commitment Against Racism:

"There are three things that will endure — faith, hope and love — and the greatest of these is love." (1 Corinthians 13:13)

Date:_____

Title of
Entry:_____

_____

My Personal Commitment Against Racism:

"There are three things that will endure — faith, hope and love — and the greatest of these is love." (1 Corinthians 13:13)

Date:_____

**Title of
Entry:**_____

_____

My Personal Commitment Against Racism:

"There are three things that will endure — faith, hope and love — and the greatest of these is love." (1 Corinthians 13:13)

Date:_____

**Title of
Entry:**_____

_____

My Personal Commitment Against Racism:

"There are three things that will endure — faith, hope and love — and the greatest of these is love." (1 Corinthians 13:13)

Date:_____

**Title of
Entry:**_____

_____

My Personal Commitment Against Racism:

"There are three things that will endure — faith, hope and love — and the greatest of these is love." (1 Corinthians 13:13)

Date:_____

**Title of
Entry:**_____

_____

My Personal Commitment Against Racism:

"There are three things that will endure — faith, hope and love — and the greatest of these is love." (1 Corinthians 13:13)

My Rays of Victory Bible Study Diary

Date:_____

Title of
Entry:_____

_____

My Personal Commitment Against Racism:

"There are three things that will endure — faith, hope and love — and the greatest of these is love." (1 Corinthians 13:13)

Date:_____

Title of
Entry:_____

_____

My Personal Commitment Against Racism:

"There are three things that will endure — faith, hope and love — and the greatest of these is love." (1 Corinthians 13:13)

My Rays of Victory Bible Study Diary

Date:_____

Title of Entry:_____

_____

My Personal Commitment Against Racism:

"There are three things that will endure — faith, hope and love — and the greatest of these is love." (1 Corinthians 13:13)

Date:_____

Title of Entry:_____

_____

My Personal Commitment Against Racism:

"There are three things that will endure — faith, hope and love — and the greatest of these is love." (1 Corinthians 13:13)

Date:_____

Title of Entry:_____

_____

My Personal Commitment Against Racism:

"There are three things that will endure — faith, hope and love — and the greatest of these is love." (1 Corinthians 13:13)

Date:_____

Title of Entry:_____

_____

My Personal Commitment Against Racism:

"There are three things that will endure — faith, hope and love — and the greatest of these is love." (1 Corinthians 13:13)

Personal Journey Entry Notes

"I have walked that long road to freedom. I have tried not to falter; I have made missteps along the way. But I have discovered the secret that after climbing a great hill, one only finds that there are many more hills to climb.

I have taken a moment here to rest, to steal a view of the glorious vista that surrounds me, to look back on the distance I have come. But I can only rest for a moment, for with freedom come responsibilities, and I dare not linger, for my long walk is not ended."

President Nelson Mandela

"There are three things that will endure — faith, hope and love — and the greatest of these is love." (1 Corinthians 13:13)

Personal Journey Entry Notes

"We have to acknowledge the progress we made, but understand that we still have a long way to go...that things are better, but still not good enough."

*****

"You're walking down the right path and you're willing to keep walking, eventually you'll make progress."

*****

"Hope – Hope in the face of difficulty. Hope in the face of uncertainty. The audacity of hope! In the end, that is God's greatest gift to us, the bedrock of this nation. A belief in things not seen. A belief that there are better days ahead."

President Barack Obama

"There are three things that will endure — faith, hope and love — and the greatest of these is love." (1 Corinthians 13:13)

Personal Notes

"There are three things that will endure — faith, hope and love — and the greatest of these is love." (1 Corinthians 13:13)

Personal Notes

"There are three things that will endure — faith, hope and love — and the greatest of these is love." (1 Corinthians 13:13)

Personal Notes

Personal Notes

"There are three things that will endure — faith, hope and love — and the greatest of these is love." (1 Corinthians 13:13)

Personal Notes

"There are three things that will endure — faith, hope and love — and the greatest of these is love." (1 Corinthians 13:13)

Personal Notes

"There are three things that will endure — faith, hope and love — and the greatest of these is love." (1 Corinthians 13:13)

Personal Notes

"There are three things that will endure—faith, hope and love—and the greatest of these is love." (1 Corinthians 13:13)

Personal Notes

"There are three things that will endure — faith, hope and love — and the greatest of these is love." (1 Corinthians 13:13)

Personal Notes

"There are three things that will endure — faith, hope and love — and the greatest of these is love." (1 Corinthians 13:13)

Personal Notes

"There are three things that will endure — faith, hope and love — and the greatest of these is love." (1 Corinthians 13:13)

Personal Notes

"There are three things that will endure — faith, hope and love — and the greatest of these is love." (1 Corinthians 13:13)

Personal Notes

"There are three things that will endure — faith, hope and love — and the greatest of these is love." (1 Corinthians 13:13)

End of Personal Notes

"There are three things that will endure — faith, hope and love — and the greatest of these is love." (1 Corinthians 13:13)

You, Me and Us!
We are all One in Jesus Christ!

"There is no longer Jew or Gentile, slave or free, male and female. For you are all one in Christ Jesus."
Galatians 3:28 NLT

"There are three things that will endure — faith, hope and love — and the greatest of these is love." (1 Corinthians 13:13)

Nailing Racism to the Cross

(Excerpt from "Nailing Racism to the Cross")

"Your race is not the purpose for your existence—it is only the shade of the physical form of your body. Your race is not your identity—your true identity is within your inner spirit; your spirit is expressed within, and through your soul and physical body it defines who and what you are. Firstly, you are made in God's excellent Image and as a believer who is born again in Jesus Christ, you have been sanctified and made holy and blameless through Him."

"At some stage in everyone's life, it becomes a matter of personal choice for every person to reject the foul spirit of racism, and to no longer acknowledge, harbor or foster that negative spirit in our heart and mind, and to make a decision not to perpetrate racist practices against others."

"The power of God's love for us and His purpose for each of our lives supersedes the power of racism or any other form of evil over our lives."

Dr. Jacyee Aniagolu-Johnson
Author, "Rays of Victory: Nailing Racism to the Cross." Christian Inspirational Non-fiction Book Series)

"There are three things that will endure — faith, hope and love — and the greatest of these is love." (1 Corinthians 13:13)

About "Nailing Racism to the Cross"
(Christian Non-Fiction)

"Rays of Victory (RAV)—Nailing Racism to the Cross" is a Christian inspirational non-fiction series with a powerful Bible-based message against racism. While racism is a sensitive subject to discuss, it is a social menace with immense negative power that needs to be tackled with spiritual warfare and wisdom. Racism has a destructive impact upon the daily lives of millions of people around the world; but we who are believers in our Lord and Savior Jesus Christ have His authority and victory over it.

For more information about the *"Nailing Racism to the Cross"* RAV Series by Marble Tower Publishing, LLC or Public Relations, please visit: marbletowerpublishing.com.

You may send your inquiries to: P.O. Box 1654, Laurel, Maryland 20725 or submit a contact request form at our RAV website: ravbookseries.com.

"There are three things that will endure —faith, hope and love —and the greatest of these is love." (1 Corinthians 13:13)

When Racism Eats Away At Your Soul
(Excerpt from "Nailing Racism to the Cross")

Racism is like a virus that eats deep into our souls to destroy our humanity. It plugs our humanity with untruth and deadens our conscience to God and the truth of His Holy Word. Racism ravages our soul and stifles the power of God from being fully expressed in and through our own lives to positively touch the lives of others. Racism pollutes our hearts. It fights our hearts and minds and attempts to detour us from God's true purpose for our lives, but true spiritual knowledge of who we are in Jesus Christ gives us clarity of God's excellent will and purpose for our lives. True spiritual knowledge stifles and suffocates any negative hold that racism may have over us.

Whether you are a practicing born again Christian, Jewish, Mormon, Moslem, New Age Believer, an Atheist, Agnostic, Buddhist, Hindu, or a follower of any other existing religions, racism is contrary to God's will and purpose for your life. It is against God's will and purpose for all other persons and all humanity. The most fundamental principal of God's creation of the human

"There are three things that will endure —faith, hope and love — and the greatest of these is love." (1 Corinthians 13:13)

being lies in the equality of all men and women, in dignity and humanity, regardless of race, ethnicity or nationality. God created every person in His excellent Image and Likeness. Therefore, the concept and practice of racism, which fosters the belief of either superiority or inferiority of an individual over another, or a group over another is false and did not originate from God. It is a lie of the enemy of our soul, the devil, whose tactics is to cause division, separation and enmity between individuals or groups of the human race. Without the true light of God dwelling in you, you could profess to be a Christian who has accepted Jesus Christ as your Lord and Savior, and yet live a life of ungodliness because your heart remains perverse in many ways. You could verbally profess to be a Christian, Jewish, Mormon, Moslem, New Age, Buddhist, Hindu, or a follower of any other faith, and still be racist. Anyone can be racist, regardless of race, ethnicity, nationality or religion.

The RAV Series deals with Christian faith and the power of God's Holy Word, the Bible, over the foul spirit of racism. The Bible tells us that the carnal state of the human heart is desperately wicked, *"The heart is deceitful above all things, and desperately wicked; Who can know it? I, the LORD,*

"There are three things that will endure — faith, hope and love — and the greatest of these is love." (1 Corinthians 13:13)

search the heart, I test the mind, even to give every man according to his ways, according to the fruit of his doings" (Jeremiah 17:9-10). It is for this reason that some of the most Bible-penetrated parts of the world still remain the most racist areas. Many individuals who profess to know Jesus Christ and God's Holy Word do not necessarily live that truth. This is why the Enemy of our soul, the devil, can continue to use racism to cause harm and division within and between Christian, non-Christian communities and all over the world. We as individuals should ask ourselves this question: "Am I prejudiced or racist against any group of people?"

So, what causes an individual or society to be prejudiced or racist or both, and to develop either inferiority or superiority complex? What motivates one individual or a group to assert superiority over another and the other to accept inferiority? The Bible says in Hosea 4:6 *"...my people are destroyed from lack of knowledge..."* When we lack true spiritual knowledge we remain in ignorance about our true self—we focus on our race and skin color rather than on our inner person. When one exists in a state of spiritual complacency or decay, devoid of the authentic truth of God's Holy Word, then one would ultimately lack true knowledge of one's self. Believing in carnal inferiority

"There are three things that will endure — faith, hope and love — and the greatest of these is love." (1 Corinthians 13:13)

or superiority signals a state of spiritual ignorance, which leads to false knowledge and belief in either carnal superiority or inferiority.

It is impossible to be in proper spiritual communion with God and feel that you are either superior or inferior to anyone. God is love and all holiness; therefore, being in proper communion with Him unveils your spiritual ignorance and brings His light of true knowledge into your being, which smothers the darkness of racist ignorance and hate. So, if you profess to be Christian, say you know God, and you are racist, you are deceiving yourself (1 John 2:9). Even though our spirits are redeemed through Jesus Christ, it is not just professing that we are Christian believers that purifies our hearts. It is actually renewing our minds with God's Holy Word (Romans 12:2; Ephesians 4:23-24), living by God's holy precepts, a Christlike life, which abhors hate, wickedness and other forms of evil including racism, all of which are contrary to God's Holy Word.

Are you racist? If you are, you know that racism is wrong; you know that it is a sin against God and an offense against your fellow human being. Therefore, it is your personal choice to continue to be racist and to perpetrate

"There are three things that will endure — faith, hope and love — and the greatest of these is love." (1 Corinthians 13:13)

racism against others. God's Holy Word tells us in Hebrews 4:12-13 (KJV): "*For the word of God is quick, and powerful, and sharper than any two-edged sword, piercing even to the dividing asunder of soul and spirit, and of the joints and marrow, and is a discerner of the thoughts and intents of the heart. Neither is there any creature that is not manifest in his sight: but all things are naked and opened unto the eyes of him with whom we have to do.*" Racism may be a secret sin because many who practice it and perpetrate and perpetuate it deny that they are racist; nonetheless every person's heart is naked and made bare to the eyes of God.

Racism is beneath any human being; Black, White, Asian, Latino and all other races and ethnicities. It is a devourer of our souls that comes only to steal, kill, and to destroy us (John 10:10a); it stifles the manifestation of God's power in our lives. Racism belittles all men and women. On the one hand, it attempts to lessen the humanity of the person who out of ignorance accepts a mark of inferiority, and on the other hand it attempts to defile the spiritual state of the other person who believes in his or her superiority. Racism attempts to deteriorate the humanity and spiritual state of both individuals when they

"There are three things that will endure — faith, hope and love — and the greatest of these is love." (1 Corinthians 13:13)

view themselves to be lower or higher than what God made them to be, relative to another person.

Racism is a form of oppression and injustice, and supports and promotes inequity. It is a form of spiritual, psychological and physical terrorism. Whether we would like to accept it or not, God frowns upon any form of oppression, injustice or inequity, subtle or overt, regardless of the source, reason or motivation behind it. Practices of racism are in direct disobedience to God's Holy Word. Therefore, racism is not just an offense against our fellow human being; it is also a sin against God Himself in whose excellent Image all humans are created.

When we allow our experiences with racism to negatively affect our hearts, minds, emotions and thoughts, it attempts to 'deface' us in our minds, and then it masks God's true Image of us in our perception of ourselves. The negative effect of racism can also be observed in the mindset, outlook, way-of-thinking, attitude and behavior of its 'wounded souls,' that is, those who are targeted by racists using discriminatory actions—those whose hearts have been crushed by the injustice of racism. Racism has the potential to break our will and make us submit to the perpetrators of such practices. However, this becomes

"There are three things that will endure — faith, hope and love — and the greatest of these is love." (1 Corinthians 13:13)

possible only if we give racists dominion—power, authority, or control—over our souls: that is our hearts, minds, thoughts, emotions, will and resolve.

While racism is designed to undermine us and make us feel less than we are, God has equipped us to take captive every racist thought or belief (2 Corinthians 10:3-6), to gain victory over every form of racism, covert or overt, by the authority He has given to us through Jesus Christ: *"And He said to them, "I saw Satan fall like lightning from heaven. Behold, I give you the authority to trample on serpents and scorpions, and over all the power of the enemy, and nothing shall by any means hurt you" (Luke 10-18-19).* Consider the foul spirit of racism a serpent and scorpion spirit and exercise the authority that God has given to you through Jesus Christ to trample and crush it. God has made each of us more than a conqueror [of racism] through Jesus Christ (Romans 8:37) who strengthens us daily.

Believe now and always that you are the victor over racism and not its victim. With the power of the Sword of the Spirit, that is, God's Holy Word, through Jesus Christ you are God's Battleaxe against the foul and obnoxious spirit of racism.

Please visit: www.marbletowerpublishing.com

"There are three things that will endure — faith, hope and love — and the greatest of these is love." (1 Corinthians 13:13)

Available:

RAYS OF VICTORY SERIES

This Book is:

My Rays of Victory

BIBLE STUDY DIARY

A Unique Diary for your Signature Penmanship as you Triumph Over Racism

∞∞∞∞∞∞∞∞ ♦ ♦ ♦ ♦ ♦ ∞∞∞∞∞∞∞∞

**By
Dr. Jacyee Aniagolu-Johnson**

First Paperback Edition:
ISBN: 978-0-9789669-4-2

"There are three things that will endure — faith, hope and love — and the greatest of these is love." (1 Corinthians 13:13)

Also Available:

RAYS OF VICTORY SERIES

150 SIGNPOSTS TO VICTORY OVER RACISM

(Volume 1)

Empowering Sign Posts for Victory Over Racism

Excerpts from "Nailing Racism to the Cross"

∞∞∞∞∞∞∞ ♦ ♦ ♦ ♦ ♦ ∞∞∞∞∞∞∞

By
Dr. Jacyee Aniagolu-Johnson

First Paperback Edition
ISBN 978-1-937230-01-2

"There are three things that will endure — faith, hope and love — and the greatest of these is love." (1 Corinthians 13:13)

RAYS OF VICTORY SERIES

150 SIGNPOSTS TO VICTORY OVER RACISM

(Volume 2)

Empowering Sign Posts for Victory Over Racism

Excerpts from "Nailing Racism to the Cross"

∞∞∞∞∞∞∞ ♦ ♦ ♦ ♦ ♦ ∞∞∞∞∞∞∞

By
Dr. Jacyee Aniagolu-Johnson

First Paperback Edition
ISBN 978-1-937230-02-9

"There are three things that will endure — faith, hope and love — and the greatest of these is love." (1 Corinthians 13:13)

RAYS OF VICTORY SERIES

150 SIGNPOSTS TO VICTORY OVER RACISM

(Volume 3)

Empowering Sign Posts for Victory Over Racism

Excerpts from "Nailing Racism to the Cross"

By
Dr. Jacyee Aniagolu-Johnson

First Paperback Edition
ISBN 978-1-937230-03-6

"There are three things that will endure — faith, hope and love — and the greatest of these is love." (1 Corinthians 13:13)

RAYS OF VICTORY SERIES

150 POWER THOUGHTS FOR VICTORY OVER RACISM

Power of a Christ-rooted Mindset Over Racism

Excerpts from "Nailing Racism to the Cross"

∞∞∞∞∞∞∞∞ ♦ ♦ ♦ ♦ ∞∞∞∞∞∞∞∞

By
Dr. Jacyee Aniagolu-Johnson

First Paperback Edition
ISBN 978-1-937-230-00-5

"There are three things that will endure — faith, hope and love — and the greatest of these is love." (1 Corinthians 13:13)

RAYS OF VICTORY SERIES

POWER THOUGHTS

Diary

FOR VICTORY OVER RACISM

Journal for Power Thoughts Against Racism [With Excerpts from "Nailing Racism to the Cross"]

By
Dr. Jacyee Aniagolu-Johnson

First Paperback Edition:
ISBN: 978-1-937230-04-3

"There are three things that will endure — faith, hope and love — and the greatest of these is love." (1 Corinthians 13:13)

RAYS OF VICTORY SERIES

WORKBOOK SERIES

FOOTPRINTS OF VICTORY OVER RACISM

In the Secret Place With God

(Volume 1)

Illuminating Daily Guideposts for God's Rays of Victory Over Racism

By
Dr. Jacyee Aniagolu-Johnson

First Paperback Edition
ISBN 978-0-9789669-5-9

"There are three things that will endure — faith, hope and love — and the greatest of these is love." (1 Corinthians 13:13)

RAYS OF VICTORY SERIES

WORKBOOK SERIES

FOOTPRINTS OF VICTORY OVER RACISM

In the Secret Place With God

(Volume 2)

Illuminating Daily Guideposts for God's Rays of Victory Over Racism

By
Dr. Jacyee Aniagolu-Johnson

First Paperback Edition
ISBN 978-0-9789669-6-6

"There are three things that will endure — faith, hope and love — and the greatest of these is love." (1 Corinthians 13:13)

RAYS OF VICTORY SERIES
ON THE HAMMOCK:
WITH THE SWORD OF THE SPIRIT
FOR INDIVIDUAL VICTORY OVER RACISM

A Meditation Journal

[40 Days of Daily Meditation]

(Volume 1)

By
Dr. Jacyee Aniagolu-Johnson

First Paperback Edition
ISBN 978-0-9789669-8-0

"There are three things that will endure — faith, hope and love — and the greatest of these is love." (1 Corinthians 13:13)

RAYS OF VICTORY SERIES

ON THE HAMMOCK:

WITH THE OIL OF GRACE

FOR INDIVIDUAL VICTORY OVER RACISM

A Meditation Journal

[40 Days of Daily Meditation]

(Volume 2)

By
Dr. Jacyee Aniagolu-Johnson

First Paperback Edition
ISBN 978-0-9789669-9-7

"There are three things that will endure — faith, hope and love — and the greatest of these is love." (1 Corinthians 13:13)

RAYS OF VICTORY SERIES

ONE ON ONE WITH GOD

FOR VICTORY OVER RACISM

Daily Prayer Conversations With God for Individual Victory Over Racism

By
Dr. Jacyee Aniagolu-Johnson

First Paperback Edition:
ISBN 978-0-9789669-7-3

"There are three things that will endure — faith, hope and love — and the greatest of these is love." (1 Corinthians 13:13)

Rays of Victory Series

Correspondence:

Please send Correspondence to:

Marble Tower Publishing

P.O. Box 1654, Laurel, Maryland 20725

OR

Submit a Contact Request Form at:

www.marbletowerpublishing.com

www.ravbookseries.com

"There are three things that will endure — faith, hope and love — and the greatest of these is love." (1 Corinthians 13:13)

"There are three things that will endure — faith, hope and love — and the greatest of these is love." (1 Corinthians 13:13)

www.ingramcontent.com/pod-product-compliance
Lightning Source LLC
LaVergne TN
LVHW051548070426
835507LV00021B/2474